# Step-by-Step Afrikaans

From Alphabet to Conversation

Earleen S.

My First Picture Book Inc.

Copyright © 2024 by My First Picture Book Inc.

All rights reserved.

No portion of this book may be reproduced in any form without written permission from the publisher or author, except as permitted by U.S. copyright law.

# Contents

1. Introduction to Afrikaans — 1
2. The Afrikaans Alphabet: Letters and Sounds — 5
3. Pronunciation Basics: Vowels and Consonants — 9
4. Common Greetings and Introductions — 13
5. Numbers and Counting in Afrikaans — 18
6. Days of the Week and Months of the Year — 23
7. Telling Time: Hours, Minutes, and Dates — 28
8. Basic Sentence Structure: Subject, Verb, Object — 33
9. Introducing Yourself and Others — 38
10. Essential Verbs: Common Actions — 43
11. Using Articles: Definite and Indefinite — 48
12. Nouns: People, Places, and Things — 52
13. Adjectives: Describing People and Things — 57
14. Forming Questions in Afrikaans — 62
15. Basic Conversation Skills: Asking and Answering — 66
16. Possessive Pronouns: Mine, Yours, Ours — 71
17. Family and Relationships Vocabulary — 75
18. Food and Dining: Everyday Vocabulary — 80
19. Colors, Shapes, and Sizes — 85
20. Talking About Weather and Seasons — 89
21. Common Expressions and Phrases — 94
22. Modal Verbs: Can, Must, Will — 99
23. Prepositions: In, On, Under, Around — 103

24. Making Comparisons: Bigger, Smaller, Faster — 107
25. Talking About Daily Activities and Routines — 111
26. Adverbs: Time, Place, and Manner — 116
27. The Present Tense: Basic Conjugation — 121
28. The Past Tense: Describing What Happened — 125
29. The Future Tense: Talking About What Will Happen — 129
30. Reflexive Verbs: Actions We Do to Ourselves — 133
31. Irregular Verbs and Their Usage — 137
32. Talking About Travel and Directions — 141
33. Health and Medical Vocabulary — 146
34. Shopping and Bargaining: Phrases and Terms — 150
35. Jobs and Professions: Talking About Work — 155
36. Afrikaans Idioms and Sayings — 160
37. Expressing Likes, Dislikes, and Preferences — 164
38. Talking About Hobbies and Interests — 169
39. Writing in Afrikaans: Simple Sentences — 174
40. Politeness and Etiquette in Afrikaans — 179
41. Talking About Hopes, Plans, and Dreams — 184
42. Cultural References and Traditions — 189
43. Formal and Informal Afrikaans: Register and Tone — 193
44. Advanced Conversation: Debates and Discussions — 198
45. Conclusion and Further Learning — 203

# Chapter 1

# Introduction to Afrikaans

## What is Afrikaans?

Afrikaans is a language spoken mainly in South Africa and Namibia. It is a very interesting language because it comes from Dutch! When Dutch settlers arrived in South Africa hundreds of years ago, their language slowly changed over time to form what we now call Afrikaans. So, if you know Dutch, Afrikaans may seem a little familiar to you. But don't worry! You don't need to know Dutch to learn Afrikaans.

Afrikaans is easy to pronounce and learn because its words often sound like they are written. This means when you see a word, it sounds almost exactly like it looks. For example, the word **kat** means "cat," and it's pronounced just like you see it. Learning a language like this can be fun and less confusing!

## Why Learn Afrikaans?

You might be wondering, "Why should I learn Afrikaans?" Well, there are many reasons!

First, it's the third most spoken language in South Africa, with millions of people speaking it every day. If you ever visit South Africa, knowing Afrikaans can help you understand the culture better, make new friends, and talk to locals. Even if you don't visit, learning Afrikaans is a great way to learn about a different part of the world from your home.

Afrikaans is also a gateway to learning other languages like Dutch and German. Since these languages are similar, once you understand Afrikaans, you might find it easier to learn them too. Plus, learning a new language helps your brain grow stronger, improves your memory, and makes you a better problem-solver.

## What We Will Teach You in This Book

In this book, we are going to start from the very basics of Afrikaans and work our way up to more complex topics. Don't worry if you've never heard a word of Afrikaans before. By the end of this book, you will know how to greet someone, have a basic conversation, talk about your favorite things, and even understand some of the grammar rules!

Here's a little overview of what we will cover:

- **Afrikaans alphabet**: The alphabet is your first step into any language. Most of the letters are the same as the English alphabet, but we'll teach you how they sound in Afrikaans.

- **Pronunciation**: You'll learn how to pronounce vowels and consonants, with lots of examples to practice.

- **Basic greetings**: For example, to say "hello," you can say **hallo** (pronounced: hah-loh), and to ask "how are you?" you can say **Hoe gaan dit?** (pronounced: hoo gahn dit?).

- **Introducing yourself**: You'll learn to say, "I am [your name]" as **Ek is [your name]** (pronounced: ek is [your name]).

- **Everyday words and phrases**: Learn words for family members, colors, numbers, and more to help you in conversations.

- **Grammar rules**: We'll make grammar fun and simple. For example, you'll learn to say "I eat an apple" as **Ek eet 'n appel** (pronounced: ek eet en ah-pel).

- **Advanced topics**: You'll even learn to talk about the past and future, saying things like what you did or what you will do.

## Understanding Afrikaans Culture

Learning a language is not just about words and grammar – it's also about understanding the culture behind it. Afrikaans is closely tied to the history and culture of South Africa. By learning this language, you are also getting a glimpse into the lives of the people who speak it.

Afrikaans is used in South African schools, businesses, and homes. It's a language that connects people, even though they might come from different backgrounds. As you learn Afrikaans, you'll also learn about South African traditions, holidays, and ways of life. For example, South Africans celebrate a holiday called **Heritage Day**, where people come together to celebrate their different cultures.

## Some Fun Facts About Afrikaans

Here are a few fun facts about Afrikaans to get you excited about learning this new language:

- Afrikaans has simpler grammar compared to many other languages, with fewer verb forms and less complex rules.

- Many Afrikaans words come from Dutch, so if you learn Dutch later, you'll recognize some words!

- Afrikaans has borrowed words from many languages, including Malay, Portuguese, and indigenous African languages, making it a unique blend of cultures.

- The word for "thanks" in Afrikaans is **Dankie** (pronounced: dun-key), which is similar to the Dutch word **Dank u**.

- Some Afrikaans words might sound funny or interesting to English speakers. For example, the word for "turtle" is **skilpad** (pronounced: skill-pahd), which literally means "shell toad"!

## How Learning Afrikaans Can Help You

Learning Afrikaans can help you in many ways. First, it's a great way to exercise your brain. Studies show that learning a new language can improve memory and concentration. It can also make it easier for you to learn other subjects like math and science.

Afrikaans can also open up new opportunities for you. If you ever travel to South Africa or Namibia, you'll be able to communicate with locals, read signs, and understand what's going on around you. You might also meet people from South Africa or Namibia in your own country, and knowing Afrikaans will help you connect with them in a special way.

Finally, learning Afrikaans can help you become more confident in yourself. The more you learn, the more you'll realize that you can accomplish big goals, even if they seem hard at first. When you finish this book, you'll have a new skill that not many people have!

## Ready to Start?

You don't need to have any experience with Afrikaans to start learning it today. Just bring your curiosity and excitement, and we'll guide you step by step through this fascinating language. Whether you want to impress your friends with new words, understand a different culture, or challenge yourself, this book will help you every step of the way.

Learning Afrikaans will be fun, and we promise to make it as simple as possible. Soon, you'll be able to read, speak, and even write in Afrikaans. Let's get started on this exciting journey together!

# Chapter 2

# The Afrikaans Alphabet: Letters and Sounds

The first step in learning any new language is to understand its alphabet. The good news is that the Afrikaans alphabet is almost identical to the English alphabet! It has 26 letters, just like the English alphabet. However, some of the letters in Afrikaans sound different than they do in English. In this chapter, we will go over the Afrikaans alphabet, how to pronounce each letter, and give you some examples of words to help you understand the sounds.

## The Afrikaans Alphabet

The Afrikaans alphabet consists of the same letters as the English alphabet:

A B C D E F G H I J K L M N O P Q R S T U V W X Y Z

As you can see, there are no extra letters to learn! But don't be fooled by the similarities—some of these letters have different sounds in Afrikaans compared to English. Let's go over how each letter is pronounced in Afrikaans, along with examples of words you might see when learning the language.

## Vowels in Afrikaans

Let's start with the vowels. In Afrikaans, the vowels are **A, E, I, O, U**, just like in English. However, they sound a bit different:

- **A** is pronounced like the "a" in **father**. For example, the word **appel** (pronounced: ah-pel), which means "apple."

- **E** is pronounced like the "e" in **bed**. An example word is **een** (pronounced: ehn), which means "one."

- **I** is pronounced like the "ee" in **see**. A word you'll see often is **is** (pronounced: ees), which means "is."

- **O** is pronounced like the "o" in **more**. For example, **oor** (pronounced: ohr), which means "ear."

- **U** is a bit tricky because it doesn't have a direct English equivalent. It sounds like "ee" but with rounded lips. For example, **uur** (pronounced: eer), which means "hour."

These vowels are very important, and learning how they sound will help you understand how words are pronounced in Afrikaans.

## Consonants in Afrikaans

Now let's move on to the consonants. Many of the consonants in Afrikaans are pronounced the same as in English, but there are a few key differences:

- **B** is pronounced the same as in English, like the "b" in **bat**. An example is **bal** (pronounced: bahl), which means "ball."

- **C** is mostly used in words borrowed from other languages and is pronounced like a "k" or "s" depending on the word. For example, **crème** (pronounced: krem) means "cream."

- **D** is pronounced like the "d" in **dog**. For example, **die** (pronounced: dee), which means "the."

- **G** is pronounced as a guttural sound, like the "ch" in the Scottish word **loch**. An example word is **goed** (pronounced: khoot), which means "good."

- **H** is pronounced like the "h" in **hat**. An example is **huis** (pronounced: hays), which means "house."

- **J** is pronounced like the "y" in **yes**. For example, **jag** (pronounced: yahkh) means "hunt."

- **K** is pronounced like the "k" in **kite**. A common word is **kat** (pronounced: kaht), which means "cat."

- **L** is pronounced like the "l" in **love**. An example is **lig** (pronounced: ligh), which means "light."

- **M** is pronounced like the "m" in **man**. A word you'll see often is **man** (pronounced: mahn), which means "man."

- **N** is pronounced like the "n" in **nice**. For example, **nee** (pronounced: nay), which means "no."

- **P** is pronounced like the "p" in **pig**. An example is **pen** (pronounced: pen), which means "pen."

- **Q** is mostly used in borrowed words and is pronounced like a "kw" sound. For example, **kwotasie** (pronounced: kwo-tah-see) means "quotation."

- **R** is pronounced with a slight roll of the tongue, similar to the Spanish "r". A word you'll often see is **rooi** (pronounced: roy), which means "red."

- **S** is pronounced like the "s" in **sun**. For example, **seun** (pronounced: soon) means "boy."

- **T** is pronounced like the "t" in **top**. An example word is **tafel** (pronounced: tah-fel), which means "table."

- **V** is pronounced like the "f" in **fun**. For example, **voet** (pronounced: foot), which means "foot."

- **W** is pronounced like the "v" in **van**. A word you'll see often is **wit** (pronounced: vit), which means "white."

- **X** is used in borrowed words and is pronounced like the "ks" in **box**. For example, **eksamen** (pronounced: ek-sah-men) means "exam."

- **Y** is pronounced like the "y" in **yes**. For example, **ys** (pronounced: ace) means "ice."

- **Z** is rare in Afrikaans but is used in borrowed words. It's pronounced like the "z" in **zoo**. For example, **zebra** (pronounced: zeh-brah) means "zebra."

## Double Letters and Diphthongs

In Afrikaans, some letters are combined to make new sounds, called diphthongs. Let's look at a few important ones:

- **aa** is pronounced like the "a" in **father**, but longer. For example, **maan** (pronounced: mahn) means "moon."

- **ee** is pronounced like the "ay" in **say**. An example is **meer** (pronounced: meer), which means "more."

- **ie** is pronounced like the "ee" in **see**. For example, **vlieg** (pronounced: fleeg), which means "fly."

- **oe** is pronounced like the "oo" in **boot**. An example is **boek** (pronounced: book), which means "book."

- **ou** is pronounced like the "ow" in **cow**. For example, **hout** (pronounced: howt), which means "wood."

## Key Points to Remember

- **Afrikaans Alphabet**: The Afrikaans alphabet has 26 letters, just like English, but some letters are pronounced differently.

- **Vowel Sounds**: Afrikaans vowels have distinct sounds, like "a" in **appel** (apple) or "u" in **uur** (hour).

- **Consonant Sounds**: Many consonants sound the same as in English, but some, like **G**, have unique pronunciations, like the guttural sound in **goed** (good).

- **Diphthongs**: Combined letters, like **aa** or **ie**, make new sounds, such as in **maan** (moon) and **vlieg** (fly).

- **Borrowed Words**: Some letters, like **C** and **Z**, appear in borrowed words and may have different sounds.

# Chapter 3

# Pronunciation Basics: Vowels and Consonants

Now that you know the Afrikaans alphabet, it's time to learn how to pronounce the letters. In this chapter, we will focus on two main parts of pronunciation: vowels and consonants. Understanding how to say these letters correctly will help you speak Afrikaans more clearly and confidently. Don't worry if it feels tricky at first—practice makes perfect!

## Vowels in Afrikaans

In Afrikaans, vowels are very important because they form the heart of almost every word. The vowels in Afrikaans are **A, E, I, O, U**, just like in English. But, as we mentioned earlier, they sound different. Let's go through each vowel one by one, so you can learn how to pronounce them.

- **A** is pronounced like the "a" in **father**. For example, the word **arm** (pronounced: ah-rm) means "arm."

- **E** is pronounced like the "e" in **bed**. For example, the word **ek** (pronounced: ek) means "I."

- **I** is pronounced like the "ee" in **see**. For example, the word **sit** (pronounced: sit) means "sit."

- **O** is pronounced like the "o" in **more**, but sometimes like the "aw" in **law**, depending on the word. An example is **om** (pronounced: om), which means "around."

- **U** is a special sound that doesn't exist in English. It's like the "ee" sound, but with rounded lips. For example, **uur** (pronounced: eer), which means "hour."

## Long and Short Vowels

In Afrikaans, vowels can be either long or short, which means you hold them for a longer or shorter amount of time. Knowing the difference between long and short vowels can change the meaning of a word!

- **Long A**: This is held a bit longer, like in the word **maan** (pronounced: mahn), which means "moon."

- **Short A**: This is shorter, like in the word **man** (pronounced: mahn), which means "man."

- **Long E**: As in **meer** (pronounced: meer), which means "more."

- **Short E**: As in **pet** (pronounced: pet), which means "cap."

As you can see, sometimes just changing how long you say a vowel can change the entire meaning of the word!

## More on Diphthongs

In addition to long and short vowels, Afrikaans has combinations of vowels called **diphthongs**. These are when two vowels blend together to make one sound. Some of the most common diphthongs in Afrikaans are:

- **aa** is pronounced like the "a" in **father**, but longer. For example, **vaar** (pronounced: fahr), which means "to sail."

- **ei** is pronounced like the "ay" in **say**. For example, **eier** (pronounced: ay-er), which means "egg."

- **oe** is pronounced like the "oo" in **boot**. For example, **boer** (pronounced: boor), which means "farmer."

- **ui** is pronounced like "ay" with a twist of "ee." An example is **huis** (pronounced: hays), which means "house."

- **ou** is pronounced like the "ow" in **cow**. For example, **blou** (pronounced: blow), which means "blue."

Learning diphthongs will make your Afrikaans pronunciation sound smoother and more natural.

## Consonants in Afrikaans

Consonants are the sounds in words that are not vowels. Most consonants in Afrikaans are pronounced just like in English, but there are some important differences. Let's go over the ones that might be new or different for you.

- **G**: In Afrikaans, the letter **G** is pronounced as a guttural sound, like the "ch" in the Scottish word **loch**. It's made in the back of your throat. For example, **groot** (pronounced: kh-root), which means "big."

- **J**: This letter sounds like the "y" in **yes**. An example is **jou** (pronounced: yow), which means "you."

- **R**: The letter **R** in Afrikaans is often rolled slightly, especially at the beginning of words. For example, **rooi** (pronounced: roy), which means "red."

- **S**: In Afrikaans, **S** is pronounced like the "s" in **sun**, never like a "z." For example, **sit** (pronounced: sit), which means "sit."

- **W**: This letter sounds like a "v" in Afrikaans. For example, **wit** (pronounced: vit), which means "white."

Getting used to these sounds may take some time, but once you know them, your Afrikaans will start to sound much more natural.

## Common Letter Combinations

In Afrikaans, there are also common letter combinations that have unique sounds. These are important to learn because they come up often in the language. Here are a few:

- **ng** is pronounced like the "ng" in **song**. For example, **lang** (pronounced: lahng), which means "long."

- **tj** is pronounced like the "ch" in **chicken**. An example is **tjop** (pronounced: chop), which means "chop" (as in a meat chop).

- **sj** is pronounced like the "sh" in **shoe**. For example, **sjokolade** (pronounced: shoh-koh-lah-duh), which means "chocolate."

Once you master these combinations, your reading and speaking will become much easier.

## Silent Letters

In Afrikaans, some letters are silent, just like in English. This means you don't pronounce them even though they are written in the word. One of the most common silent letters is **D** at the end of some words:

- In the word **hond** (pronounced: hont), meaning "dog," the **D** is silent, so you only hear the "t" sound at the end.

- The same is true for **grond** (pronounced: gront), meaning "ground."

It's important to remember these silent letters when learning new words!

## Special Sounds in Afrikaans

Afrikaans also has a few unique sounds that you won't find in English. Here are two special sounds to pay attention to:

- **Schwa sound**: This is a short, weak sound like the "a" in **sofa**. You'll often hear it at the end of words, like in **water** (pronounced: vah-tuh), which means "water."

- **Guttural G**: As mentioned before, the **G** is a harsh sound made at the back of the throat. This can take some time to get used to, but with practice, it will become easier.

## Key Points to Remember

- **Afrikaans Vowels**: Vowels in Afrika ans can be long or short, and they sometimes sound different from English vowels, like the "u" in **uur** (hour).

- **Diphthongs**: Diphthongs combine two vowels to make one sound, such as **ou** in **blou** (blue).

- **Consonants**: Some consonants, like **G** and **W**, sound different in Afrikaans than in English. Practice these to improve your pronunciation.

- **Letter Combinations**: Common letter combinations, like **ng** and **tj**, have special sounds in Afrikaans that you need to learn.

- **Silent Letters**: Watch out for silent letters, like the silent **D** in **hond** (dog).

# Chapter 4

# Common Greetings and Introductions

Now that you know the Afrikaans alphabet and some basic sounds, it's time to learn how to greet people and introduce yourself in Afrikaans. Greetings and introductions are some of the first things you need to know when learning any new language because they help you start conversations and make new friends. In this chapter, we will go over common greetings and how to introduce yourself in Afrikaans, along with examples to help you practice.

## Basic Greetings

In Afrikaans, greetings are simple and straightforward. Let's start with a few common ways to say "hello" and "goodbye."

- **Hello**: In Afrikaans, you can say **hallo** (pronounced: hah-loh). It's just like the English word "hello" but with a slightly different sound. You can use **hallo** in both formal and informal situations.

- **Good morning**: To say "good morning," you can say **goeie môre** (pronounced: gooy-uh mo-ruh). This is a polite way to greet someone in the morning.

- **Good afternoon**: If you want to say "good afternoon," you can say **goeie middag** (pronounced: gooy-uh mid-dahkh). You use this greeting after noon but before evening.

- **Good evening**: To greet someone in the evening, you say **goeie naand** (pronounced: gooy-uh nahnt). This is the same as saying "good evening" in English.

- **Goodbye**: To say "goodbye" in Afrikaans, you can say **totsiens** (pronounced: tot-seens). This word literally means "until we see each other again."

As you can see, the word **goeie** (pronounced: gooy-uh) is used in a lot of greetings. It means "good," so when you say **goeie môre** or **goeie naand**, you're literally saying "good morning" or "good evening."

## Asking How Someone Is

After greeting someone, it's common to ask how they are. In Afrikaans, the phrase for asking "how are you?" is:

- **Hoe gaan dit met jou?** (pronounced: hoo gahn dit met yow?) – This means "how are you?" You can use this question when talking to friends, family, or anyone you're meeting for the first time.

If someone asks you **Hoe gaan dit met jou?**, you can respond in a few different ways depending on how you're feeling:

- **Dit gaan goed, dankie** (pronounced: dit gahn khoot, dun-key) – This means "I am fine, thank you."
- **Ek is moeg** (pronounced: ek is mookh) – This means "I am tired."
- **Ek is siek** (pronounced: ek is seek) – This means "I am sick."

After giving your response, it's polite to ask the other person how they are. You can simply say:

- **En jy?** (pronounced: en yay?) – This means "and you?"

## Introducing Yourself

Once you've greeted someone and asked how they are, the next step is to introduce yourself. In Afrikaans, introducing yourself is easy. Here's how you can do it:

- **Ek is [your name]** (pronounced: ek is [your name]) – This means "I am [your name]."

For example, if your name is Sarah, you would say:

- **Ek is Sarah** (pronounced: ek is sah-rah)

If you want to say where you are from, you can use this sentence:

- **Ek kom van [place]** (pronounced: ek kom fahn [place]) – This means "I am from [place]."

For example, if you are from New York, you would say:

- **Ek kom van New York** (pronounced: ek kom fahn new york)

If you want to say how old you are, you can say:

- **Ek is [your age] jaar oud** (pronounced: ek is [your age] yah-r owt) – This means "I am [your age] years old."

For example, if you are 12 years old, you would say:

- **Ek is 12 jaar oud** (pronounced: ek is twahlf yah-r owt)

## Introducing Someone Else

If you're with a friend and want to introduce them to someone, you can say:

- **Dit is my vriend [friend's name]** (pronounced: dit is may freend [friend's name]) – This means "This is my friend [friend's name]."

For example, if your friend's name is John, you would say:

- **Dit is my vriend John** (pronounced: dit is may freend john)

If you are introducing a female friend, you can use the word **vriendin** (pronounced: freen-din), which means "female friend."

## Polite Phrases to Use in Conversations

When meeting new people, it's important to use polite phrases. Here are some useful ones:

- **Baie dankie** (pronounced: bah-yuh dun-key) – This means "thank you very much."
- **Asseblief** (pronounced: ah-suh-bleef) – This means "please."
- **Verskoon my** (pronounced: fer-skoon may) – This means "excuse me."
- **Dis 'n plesier** (pronounced: dis en pleh-seer) – This means "you're welcome."

Using these polite words will make your conversations friendlier and more respectful.

## Yes and No

In Afrikaans, the words for "yes" and "no" are very easy to learn. Here's how to say them:

- **Yes**: In Afrikaans, you say **ja** (pronounced: yah).

- **No**: To say "no," you say **nee** (pronounced: nay).

If someone asks you a question, you can respond with **ja** or **nee**, depending on your answer.

## Small Talk in Afrikaans

Small talk is a way to have light, friendly conversations with people you've just met. Here are some simple phrases you can use for small talk in Afrikaans:

- **Hoe lyk die weer?** (pronounced: hoo layk dee vehr) – This means "How's the weather?"

- **Waar bly jy?** (pronounced: vah-r blay yay) – This means "Where do you live?"

- **Wat is jou gunsteling kos?** (pronounced: vat is yow khuns-te-ling kaws) – This means "What is your favorite food?"

These are great conversation starters, and they can help you get to know someone better.

## Practice Example Conversation

Here's a quick example of how a simple conversation in Afrikaans might go:

- **Person 1:** Hallo! Hoe gaan dit met jou? (Hello! How are you?)

- **Person 2:** Dit gaan goed, dankie. En jy? (I'm fine, thank you. And you?)

- **Person 1:** Ek is goed, dankie. Ek is Sarah. (I'm fine, thank you. I am Sarah.)

- **Person 2:** Ek is John. Dit is lekker om jou te ontmoet. (I am John. It's nice to meet you.)

This is just a simple conversation, but it covers greetings, introductions, and polite phrases, all in one!

## Key Points to Remember

- **Common Greetings**: Greet people with **hallo** (hello) or **goeie môre** (good morning) depending on the time of day.

- **Asking How Someone Is**: Ask **Hoe gaan dit met jou?** (How are you?), and reply with **Dit gaan goed, dankie** (I'm fine, thank you).

- **Introducing Yourself**: Say **Ek is [your name]** (I am [your name]) and **Ek kom van**

**[place]** (I am from [place]).

- **Polite Phrases**: Use **asseblief** (please) and **baie dankie** (thank you very much) to be polite.

- **Yes and No**: Say **ja** (yes) or **nee** (no) when answering questions.

# Chapter 5

# Numbers and Counting in Afrikaans

Numbers are an important part of any language, and in Afrikaans, learning how to count is simple and fun. In this chapter, we will go over how to count in Afrikaans, from 1 to 100 and beyond, and show you how numbers are used in everyday life. By the end of this chapter, you will be able to use numbers in conversations, talk about your age, tell the time, and more!

## Counting from 1 to 10

Let's start with the basics: numbers 1 to 10. These are the foundation for everything else, and once you know these, you'll find it easier to count to higher numbers. Here's how you count from 1 to 10 in Afrikaans:

- **1 – een** (pronounced: ehn)
- **2 – twee** (pronounced: tway)
- **3 – drie** (pronounced: dree)
- **4 – vier** (pronounced: feer)
- **5 – vyf** (pronounced: fayf)
- **6 – ses** (pronounced: ses)
- **7 – sewe** (pronounced: see-wuh)
- **8 – agt** (pronounced: ahkt)
- **9 – nege** (pronounced: nee-ghuh)

- **10 – tien** (pronounced: teen)

Practice saying these numbers out loud. Notice that some of them sound similar to English, while others are quite different. For example, **een** (1) sounds a bit like "one," and **twee** (2) sounds a lot like "two." However, numbers like **vyf** (5) and **sewe** (7) might be new to you.

## Counting from 11 to 20

Once you can count from 1 to 10, the next step is counting from 11 to 20. These numbers are also very important because they help you form larger numbers later on. Here's how you count from 11 to 20 in Afrikaans:

- **11 – elf** (pronounced: elf)
- **12 – twaalf** (pronounced: twahlf)
- **13 – dertien** (pronounced: der-teen)
- **14 – veertien** (pronounced: feer-teen)
- **15 – vyftien** (pronounced: fayf-teen)
- **16 – sestien** (pronounced: ses-teen)
- **17 – sewentien** (pronounced: see-wen-teen)
- **18 – agtien** (pronounced: ahk-teen)
- **19 – negentien** (pronounced: nee-ghen-teen)
- **20 – twintig** (pronounced: twin-tukh)

You'll notice that numbers 13 to 19 in Afrikaans follow a pattern: they all end in **-tien**, which means "teen." This is very similar to English. So, **dertien** is "thirteen," **veertien** is "fourteen," and so on. The number 20 is **twintig**, which sounds a bit like "twenty."

## Counting in Tens: 30, 40, 50, and More

Now that you know how to count to 20, it's time to learn the tens. These numbers help you count higher, and they're used to talk about things like prices, age, and time. Here's how you count in tens in Afrikaans:

- **30 – dertig** (pronounced: der-tukh)

- **40 – veertig** (pronounced: feer-tukh)
- **50 – vyftig** (pronounced: fayf-tukh)
- **60 – sestig** (pronounced: ses-tukh)
- **70 – sewentig** (pronounced: see-wen-tukh)
- **80 – tagtig** (pronounced: tahkh-tukh)
- **90 – negentig** (pronounced: nee-ghen-tukh)
- **100 – honderd** (pronounced: hon-derd)

In Afrikaans, the pattern is simple: you add **-tig** to the base number to form the tens. For example, **dertig** (30) comes from **dertien** (13), and **veertig** (40) comes from **veertien** (14).

## Forming Larger Numbers

Now that you know the tens, you can form larger numbers easily. Just like in English, you combine the tens and ones to make numbers like 21, 32, 54, and so on. Here's how to do it:

- **21 – een-en-twintig** (pronounced: ehn-en-twin-tukh) – This means "twenty-one."
- **32 – twee-en-dertig** (pronounced: tway-en-der-tukh) – This means "thirty-two."
- **54 – vier-en-vyftig** (pronounced: feer-en-fayf-tukh) – This means "fifty-four."

To form numbers like these, you use the pattern **[ones] + en + [tens]**. For example, **21** is **een-en-twintig**, which means "one and twenty." This is a little different from English, where we say "twenty-one" instead of "one and twenty," but you'll get used to it quickly.

## Counting Higher: Hundreds and Beyond

In Afrikaans, counting beyond 100 is just as easy. Here's how you do it:

- **100 – honderd** (pronounced: hon-derd) – This means "one hundred."
- **200 – tweehonderd** (pronounced: tway-hon-derd) – This means "two hundred."
- **1,000 – duisend** (pronounced: doy-sent) – This means "one thousand."

When forming larger numbers, you simply combine the words you already know. For example, **154** would be **honderd vier-en-vyftig** (pronounced: hon-derd feer-en-fayf-tukh), which means "one hundred and fifty-four."

## Using Numbers in Everyday Life

Now that you know how to count in Afrikaans, let's see how numbers are used in everyday life. Whether you're talking about your age, telling the time, or shopping, numbers play a big role in conversations. Here are some examples of how to use numbers in real-life situations:

## Talking About Your Age

To say how old you are, you can use this sentence:

- **Ek is [your age] jaar oud** (pronounced: ek is [your age] yah-r owt) – This means "I am [your age] years old."

For example, if you are 12 years old, you would say:

- **Ek is 12 jaar oud** (pronounced: ek is twahlf yah-r owt)

## Telling the Time

Telling the time in Afrikaans is also easy once you know the numbers. Here's how you can say what time it is:

- **Dit is eenuur** (pronounced: dit is ehn-oor) – This means "It is one o'clock."
- **Dit is tien-oor-vyf** (pronounced: teen ohr fayf) – This means "It is ten past five."

## Shopping and Prices

When you go shopping, numbers are important for understanding prices. In Afrikaans, prices are often written the same way as in English, but here's how you might say the price of something:

- **Dit kos vyf-en-twintig rand** (pronounced: fayf-en-twin-tukh rahnd) – This means "It costs twenty-five rand."

**Rand** is the currency of South Africa, and you will often hear prices in rand when shopping.

## Ordinal Numbers: First, Second, Third...

In addition to regular numbers, Afrikaans also has ordinal numbers, which are used to say things like "first," "second," "third," and so on. Here's how you say the first few ordinal numbers in Afrikaans:

- **1st – eerste** (pronounced: eer-stuh)
- **2nd – tweede** (pronounced: tway-duh)
- **3rd – derde** (pronounced: der-duh)

These ordinal numbers are useful when talking about order, such as who came in first place in a race, or what the date is (like the first of May).

## Key Points to Remember

- **Counting to 10**: Learn the numbers from 1 to 10 first, as they form the basis for all other numbers.

- **Counting to 20**: Numbers 11 to 20 in Afrikaans follow a similar pattern to English, with **-tien** at the end for "teen" numbers.

- **Forming Larger Numbers**: Combine tens and ones using **en** (and), like **een-en-twintig** (21).

- **Counting in Hundreds and Thousands**: Numbers over 100 are formed by combining the hundreds and ones, such as **honderd en een** (101).

- **Ordinal Numbers**: Use ordinal numbers like **eerste** (first) and **tweede** (second) when talking about order.

# Chapter 6

# Days of the Week and Months of the Year

Knowing how to talk about days of the week and months of the year is very important in any language. In Afrikaans, the words for the days and months are quite similar to English, making them easy to learn and remember. In this chapter, we will go over how to say the days of the week, the months of the year, and how to use them in sentences. By the end, you'll be able to talk about when things happen, make plans, and understand dates.

## Days of the Week in Afrikaans

Let's start by learning how to say the days of the week. In Afrikaans, there are seven days just like in English, and most of them sound pretty similar. Here's a list of the days:

- **Monday – Maandag** (pronounced: mahn-dahkh)

- **Tuesday – Dinsdag** (pronounced: dins-dahkh)

- **Wednesday – Woensdag** (pronounced: voons-dahkh)

- **Thursday – Donderdag** (pronounced: don-der-dahkh)

- **Friday – Vrydag** (pronounced: fray-dahkh)

- **Saturday – Saterdag** (pronounced: sah-ter-dahkh)

- **Sunday – Sondag** (pronounced: son-dahkh)

As you can see, the word **dag** (pronounced: dahkh), which means "day," is added to the end of each day. So, for example, **Maandag** means "Monday," and **Dinsdag** means "Tuesday." Let's go through each day:

- **Maandag**: This is the first day of the week, and it sounds similar to "Monday."

- **Dinsdag**: Tuesday in Afrikaans, pronounced dins-dahkh, is similar to the English word "Tuesday."

- **Woensdag**: Wednesday in Afrikaans starts with a "w" but is pronounced with a "v" sound: voons-dahkh.

- **Donderdag**: Thursday is called don-der-dahkh in Afrikaans. Notice how the first part sounds like "donder," which means "thunder" in Afrikaans.

- **Vrydag**: Friday in Afrikaans is pronounced fray-dahkh, which is easy to remember because it sounds like "Friday."

- **Saterdag**: Saturday is pronounced sah-ter-dahkh, similar to "Saturday" in English.

- **Sondag**: Sunday is pronounced son-dahkh, very similar to "Sunday" in English.

## Using Days of the Week in Sentences

Now that you know the days of the week, let's see how to use them in sentences. In Afrikaans, you can talk about days just like you do in English. Here are a few examples:

- **Vandag is Maandag** (pronounced: fan-dahkh is mahn-dahkh) – This means "Today is Monday."

- **Ek sal jou Dinsdag sien** (pronounced: ek sahl yow dins-dahkh seen) – This means "I will see you on Tuesday."

- **Ons gaan op Saterdag speel** (pronounced: ohns khahn op sah-ter-dahkh spayl) – This means "We are going to play on Saturday."

When talking about an event happening on a certain day, you use the word **op** (pronounced: op), which means "on." For example, **op Maandag** means "on Monday."

## Months of the Year in Afrikaans

Just like in English, there are twelve months in a year in Afrikaans. Many of the names for the months in Afrikaans are very similar to English, so you'll find them easy to learn. Here are the months of the year in Afrikaans:

- **January – Januarie** (pronounced: yahn-yoo-ah-ree)

- **February – Februarie** (pronounced: fay-broo-ah-ree)

- **March – Maart** (pronounced: mahrt)

- **April – April** (pronounced: ah-pril)

- **May – Mei** (pronounced: may)

- **June – Junie** (pronounced: yoo-nee)

- **July – Julie** (pronounced: yoo-lee)

- **August – Augustus** (pronounced: ow-khus-tus)

- **September – September** (pronounced: sep-tem-ber)

- **October – Oktober** (pronounced: ok-toh-ber)

- **November – November** (pronounced: noh-vem-ber)

- **December – Desember** (pronounced: deh-sem-ber)

Many of the months sound almost exactly like the English months, which makes them easier to remember. For example, **Januarie** (January), **Februarie** (February), and **September** are pronounced very similarly in both languages.

## Using Months in Sentences

Now that you know the months of the year, let's see how you can use them in everyday sentences. Here are some examples:

- **Ek is in Januarie gebore** (pronounced: ek is in yahn-yoo-ah-ree khe-boh-reh) – This means "I was born in January."

- **My verjaarsdag is in Mei** (pronounced: may fer-yahrs-dahkh is in may) – This means "My birthday is in May."

- **Ons gaan in Desember vakansie hou** (pronounced: ohns khahn in deh-sem-ber fah-kahn-see yow) – This means "We are going on vacation in December."

When talking about something happening in a specific month, you use the word **in** (pronounced: in), which is the same as in English. For example, **in Maart** means "in March," and **in April** means "in April."

## Seasons in Afrikaans

In addition to the days of the week and months of the year, it's useful to know the seasons in Afrikaans. South Africa has four seasons just like the USA, but because it's in the southern hemisphere, the seasons are opposite. Here are the Afrikaans words for the four seasons:

- **Summer – Somer** (pronounced: soh-mer)
- **Autumn – Herfs** (pronounced: herfs)
- **Winter – Winter** (pronounced: vin-ter)
- **Spring – Lente** (pronounced: len-tuh)

For example, when it's winter in the USA, it's summer in South Africa. If you want to say that something happens during a certain season, you can use the word **in**, just like with months. Here's an example:

- **Ons gaan in die somer swem** (pronounced: ohns khahn in dee soh-mer swim) – This means "We are going to swim in the summer."

## Talking About Dates

In Afrikaans, talking about dates is very similar to English. You just need to know the day and the month. Here's how to say the date in Afrikaans:

- **Vandag is die eerste April** (pronounced: fan-dahkh is dee eer-stuh ah-pril) – This means "Today is the first of April."

When saying the date, the number comes first, followed by the month. For example, **die tweede Maart** means "the second of March," and **die tiende Mei** means "the tenth of May."

## Key Points to Remember

- **Days of the Week**: Days of the week in Afrikaans end with **-dag**, such as **Maandag** (Monday) and **Dinsdag** (Tuesday).

- **Months of the Year**: Many months in Afrikaans sound similar to their English counterparts, like **Januarie** (January) and **April** (April).

- **Using "Op" and "In"**: Use **op** (on) when talking about days and **in** when talking about months or seasons.

- **Seasons**: The four seasons in Afrikaans are **somer** (summer), **herfs** (autumn), **winter** (winter), and **lente** (spring).

- **Talking About Dates**: When saying a date, you use the number first and then the month, like **die tweede Maart** (the second of March).

# Chapter 7

# Telling Time: Hours, Minutes, and Dates

Being able to tell time is an important skill in any language, and in Afrikaans, it's quite easy once you understand the basics. In this chapter, we'll go through how to tell the time, talk about hours and minutes, and use dates in conversations. By the end of this chapter, you'll be able to ask for the time, tell someone what time it is, and even discuss specific dates. Let's get started!

## Asking for the Time

If you want to know what time it is, you can ask:

- **Hoe laat is dit?** (pronounced: hoo laht is dit?) – This means "What time is it?"

The word **laat** (pronounced: laht) means "late," but in this question, it's used to ask about the time of day. This is a simple phrase you can use whenever you need to ask the time.

## Telling the Time: Hours

To answer someone when they ask the time, you need to know how to say the hours in Afrikaans. Here's how to say each hour:

- **1 o'clock – eenuur** (pronounced: ehn-oor)

- **2 o'clock – twee-uur** (pronounced: tway-oor)

- **3 o'clock – drie-uur** (pronounced: dree-oor)

- **4 o'clock – vier-uur** (pronounced: feer-oor)

- **5 o'clock – vyf-uur** (pronounced: fayf-oor)

- **6 o'clock – sesuur** (pronounced: ses-oor)
- **7 o'clock – sewe-uur** (pronounced: see-wuh-oor)
- **8 o'clock – agtuur** (pronounced: ahkt-oor)
- **9 o'clock – nege-uur** (pronounced: nee-ghuh-oor)
- **10 o'clock – tienuur** (pronounced: teen-oor)
- **11 o'clock – elfuur** (pronounced: elf-oor)
- **12 o'clock – twaalfuur** (pronounced: twahlf-oor)

In Afrikaans, the word **uur** means "hour" or "o'clock," so you combine the number with **uur** to tell the time. For example, **vier-uur** means "four o'clock."

## Minutes in Afrikaans

In Afrikaans, you can talk about minutes in two main ways: minutes past the hour or minutes before the next hour. Let's look at both.

## Minutes Past the Hour

To talk about minutes after the hour, you say the number of minutes followed by the word **oor** (meaning "past") and the hour. Here are some examples:

- **10:05 – vyf oor tien** (pronounced: fayf ohr teen) – This means "five past ten."
- **3:15 – vyftien oor drie** (pronounced: fayf-teen ohr dree) – This means "fifteen past three."
- **7:20 – twintig oor sewe** (pronounced: twin-tukh ohr see-wuh) – This means "twenty past seven."

The word **oor** is important because it tells you how many minutes have passed after the hour.

## Minutes to the Next Hour

If you want to say how many minutes are left until the next hour, you use the word **voor** (meaning "before"). Here are some examples:

- **11:55 – vyf voor twaalf** (pronounced: fayf fohr twahlf) – This means "five to twelve."

- **4:45 – vyftien voor vyf** (pronounced: fayf-teen fohr fayf) – This means "fifteen to five."
- **6:50 – tien voor sewe** (pronounced: teen fohr see-wuh) – This means "ten to seven."

Here, the word **voor** helps indicate how many minutes remain until the next hour.

## Half Past and Quarter Past

In Afrikaans, you can also talk about time using "half past" or "quarter past" and "quarter to." These phrases are very common, especially when talking about more general times.

- **3:30 – halfvier** (pronounced: half-feer) – This means "half past three."
- **7:15 – kwart oor sewe** (pronounced: kwart ohr see-wuh) – This means "quarter past seven."
- **8:45 – kwart voor nege** (pronounced: kwart fohr nee-ghuh) – This means "quarter to nine."

In Afrikaans, **halfvier** means "half of four," which refers to 3:30, halfway to four o'clock. The word **kwart** (pronounced: kwart) means "quarter," and it's used when talking about fifteen minutes past or to the hour.

## Talking About Dates

Now that you know how to tell time, let's learn how to talk about dates. In Afrikaans, dates are spoken in a way similar to English. Here's how you can say a date:

- **Vandag is die eerste Januarie** (pronounced: fan-dahkh is dee eer-stuh yahn-yoo-ah-ree) – This means "Today is the first of January."

The word **eerste** (pronounced: eer-stuh) means "first," and you use it to talk about the first day of the month. Similarly, **tweede** (pronounced: tway-duh) means "second," and **derde** (pronounced: der-duh) means "third." Here are more examples:

- **Die tweede April** (pronounced: dee tway-duh ah-pril) – This means "the second of April."
- **Die tiende Mei** (pronounced: dee teen-duh may) – This means "the tenth of May."
- **Die twintigste Desember** (pronounced: dee twin-tukh-stuh deh-sem-ber) – This means "the twentieth of December."

# TELLING TIME: HOURS, MINUTES, AND DATES

When saying dates in Afrikaans, the number comes first, followed by the month. You also use the word **die** (pronounced: dee), which means "the," before saying the date.

## Using "AM" and "PM" in Afrikaans

In Afrikaans, there isn't a specific equivalent for "AM" and "PM" like in English. Instead, people use the time of day to explain whether it's morning, afternoon, or evening. Here are some phrases you can use:

- **In die oggend** (pronounced: in dee oh-khent) – This means "in the morning."

- **In die middag** (pronounced: in dee mid-dahkh) – This means "in the afternoon."

- **In die aand** (pronounced: in dee ahnt) – This means "in the evening."

So, if you want to say "10 o'clock in the morning," you would say **tienuur in die oggend** (pronounced: teen-oor in dee oh-khent). For "7 o'clock in the evening," you would say **sewe-uur in die aand** (pronounced: see-wuh-oor in dee ahnt).

## Talking About Specific Times

Sometimes, you'll need to be more specific when talking about time. In Afrikaans, you can use the same structure to say exactly when something is happening. Here are some examples:

- **Ons gaan om vyfuur vertrek** (pronounced: ohns khahn om fayf-oor fer-trek) – This means "We are leaving at five o'clock."

- **Die vergadering is om drie-uur** (pronounced: dee fehr-ghah-der-ing is om dree-oor) – This means "The meeting is at three o'clock."

The word **om** (pronounced: om) means "at," so you use it when talking about what time something is happening.

## Key Points to Remember

- **Asking for the Time**: Use **Hoe laat is dit?** to ask "What time is it?" in Afrikaans.

- **Telling Time with Hours**: Combine the number and **uur** to say the time, like **drie-uur** (three o'clock).

- **Talking About Minutes**: Use **oor** for minutes past the hour and **voor** for minutes before the next hour, like **vyf oor tien** (five past ten).

- **Half Past and Quarter Past**: Say **halfvier** (half past three) or **kwart oor sewe** (quarter past seven) to talk about more general times.

- **Using AM and PM**: Use phrases like **in die oggend** (in the morning) and **in die aand** (in the evening) instead of "AM" and "PM."

# Chapter 8

# Basic Sentence Structure: Subject, Verb, Object

Every language has its own rules for how sentences are put together, and Afrikaans is no different. To speak and write in Afrikaans, you need to know the basic sentence structure. In this chapter, we'll learn about the most important parts of a sentence: the subject, the verb, and the object. These are the building blocks that will help you create sentences and communicate clearly in Afrikaans.

## What is a Subject?

The subject of a sentence is the person, place, or thing that is doing the action. In other words, it is who or what the sentence is about. Let's look at some examples in Afrikaans:

- **Ek** (pronounced: ek) – This means "I."

- **Hy** (pronounced: hay) – This means "he."

- **Sy** (pronounced: say) – This means "she."

- **Ons** (pronounced: ohns) – This means "we."

- **Hulle** (pronounced: huh-luh) – This means "they."

These are all examples of subjects. They tell us who is doing the action in a sentence. In Afrikaans, the subject usually comes first in a sentence, just like in English. For example:

- **Ek eet** (pronounced: ek eet) – This means "I eat."

- **Hy loop** (pronounced: hay lohp) – This means "He walks."

In both sentences, **Ek** and **Hy** are the subjects because they are doing the action.

## What is a Verb?

The verb is the action word in a sentence. It tells us what the subject is doing. Here are some examples of verbs in Afrikaans:

- **eet** (pronounced: eet) – This means "eat."
- **lees** (pronounced: lees) – This means "read."
- **swem** (pronounced: swim) – This means "swim."
- **speel** (pronounced: speel) – This means "play."

The verb usually comes after the subject in Afrikaans. Let's look at a few examples:

- **Sy lees** (pronounced: say lees) – This means "She reads."
- **Ons swem** (pronounced: ohns swim) – This means "We swim."

In these sentences, **lees** and **swem** are the verbs because they describe the actions of the subjects. The subject tells us who is doing the action, and the verb tells us what the action is.

## What is an Object?

The object in a sentence is the thing that the action is being done to. In other words, it's what is affected by the verb. Here are some examples of objects in Afrikaans:

- **kos** (pronounced: kaws) – This means "food."
- **boek** (pronounced: book) – This means "book."
- **bal** (pronounced: bahl) – This means "ball."

In Afrikaans, the object usually comes after the verb, just like in English. Let's look at some examples:

- **Ek eet kos** (pronounced: ek eet kaws) – This means "I eat food."
- **Hy lees 'n boek** (pronounced: hay lees en book) – This means "He reads a book."
- **Ons speel met die bal** (pronounced: ohns speel met dee bahl) – This means "We play with the ball."

In these sentences, the object is **kos**, **boek**, and **bal** because they are the things that are being eaten, read, and played with.

## The Basic Sentence Structure: Subject, Verb, Object

Now that we know what subjects, verbs, and objects are, let's put them together. In Afrikaans, the basic sentence structure is **subject + verb + object**. Here are some examples:

- **Ek drink water** (pronounced: ek drink vah-ter) – This means "I drink water."

- **Sy skryf 'n brief** (pronounced: say skrayf en bree-f) – This means "She writes a letter."

- **Hulle eet vrugte** (pronounced: huh-luh eet frukh-tuh) – This means "They eat fruit."

In these sentences, the subject comes first, followed by the verb, and then the object. This is the basic pattern that most Afrikaans sentences follow.

## Changing the Order in Questions

When you ask a question in Afrikaans, the order of the words can change. In a question, the verb often comes before the subject. For example:

- **Eet jy kos?** (pronounced: eet yay kaws?) – This means "Do you eat food?"

- **Lees sy 'n boek?** (pronounced: lees say en book?) – This means "Does she read a book?"

In these sentences, the verb comes first, followed by the subject, and then the object. Notice how the order is different from a regular sentence.

## Negative Sentences in Afrikaans

In Afrikaans, when you want to say something negative, you use the word **nie** (pronounced: nee) to mean "not." Here's how you make a sentence negative:

- **Ek lees nie** (pronounced: ek lees nee) – This means "I do not read."

- **Hy eet nie kos nie** (pronounced: hay eet nee kaws nee) – This means "He does not eat food."

Notice that **nie** is used twice in the second sentence, which is common in Afrikaans negative sentences. The first **nie** comes after the verb, and the second **nie** comes at the end of the sentence.

## Common Phrases Using Subject, Verb, Object

Here are some simple sentences that follow the subject-verb-object structure, which you can use in everyday conversations:

- **Ek leer Afrikaans** (pronounced: ek layr ah-free-kahns) – This means "I learn Afrikaans."

- **Ons kyk televisie** (pronounced: ohns kayk tell-eh-vee-see) – This means "We watch television."

- **Sy maak kos** (pronounced: say mahk kaws) – This means "She makes food."

These sentences follow the simple pattern of subject + verb + object, making it easy to form your own sentences.

## Expanding Your Sentences

Once you understand the basic sentence structure, you can start adding more details to your sentences. For example, you can include where or when something happens:

- **Ek eet kos in die kombuis** (pronounced: ek eet kaws in dee kom-bays) – This means "I eat food in the kitchen."

- **Ons speel sokker elke dag** (pronounced: ohns speel soh-ker el-kuh dahkh) – This means "We play soccer every day."

In these examples, extra information is added about where (**in die kombuis**) and when (**elke dag**) something happens.

## Key Points to Remember

- **Subject First**: The subject is who or what the sentence is about, like **Ek** (I) or **Sy** (She).

- **Verb Comes Next**: The verb tells what the subject is doing, like **eet** (eat) or **swem (swim).**

- **Object Comes Last:** The object is the thing affected by the verb, like **kos** (food) or **boek** (book).

- **Word Order in Questions:** In questions, the verb often comes before the subject, like **Lees sy 'n boek**? (Does she read a book?).

- **Negative Sentences:** To make a sentence negative, use **nie** after the verb and at the end of the sentence, like **Hy eet nie kos nie** (He does not eat food).

# Chapter 9

# Introducing Yourself and Others

One of the first things you learn when speaking a new language is how to introduce yourself and others. In Afrikaans, introductions are simple and easy to learn. In this chapter, we'll cover how to introduce yourself, how to talk about where you're from, and how to introduce other people. By the end, you'll be able to confidently introduce yourself and others in Afrikaans.

## Introducing Yourself

The most basic way to introduce yourself in Afrikaans is by saying your name. To do this, you use the phrase:

- **Ek is [your name]** (pronounced: ek is [your name]) – This means "I am [your name]."

For example, if your name is Sarah, you would say:

- **Ek is Sarah** (pronounced: ek is sah-rah)

Similarly, if your name is John, you would say:

- **Ek is John** (pronounced: ek is john)

This is the most direct way to tell someone your name. It's simple and polite, and it's the phrase you'll use in most situations.

## Where You're From

After you tell someone your name, you may want to tell them where you are from. To do this in Afrikaans, you use the sentence:

- **Ek kom van [place]** (pronounced: ek kom fahn [place]) – This means "I am from [place]."

For example, if you are from New York, you would say:

- **Ek kom van New York** (pronounced: ek kom fahn new york)

If you are from a different city or country, just replace "New York" with the name of your hometown or country. Here are a few more examples:

- **Ek kom van Los Angeles** (pronounced: ek kom fahn lohs an-juh-lis) – "I am from Los Angeles."
- **Ek kom van Suid-Afrika** (pronounced: ek kom fahn sayt ah-fri-kah) – "I am from South Africa."

In these sentences, **Ek kom** means "I come," and **van** means "from." It's a simple way to tell someone where you're from.

## Talking About Your Age

If you want to tell someone how old you are, you can use this phrase:

- **Ek is [age] jaar oud** (pronounced: ek is [age] yah-r owt) – This means "I am [age] years old."

For example, if you are 12 years old, you would say:

- **Ek is 12 jaar oud** (pronounced: ek is twahlf yah-r owt)

Here, **jaar** means "year" and **oud** means "old." So when you say **Ek is 12 jaar oud**, you're literally saying "I am 12 years old."

## Introducing Someone Else

If you're with a friend or family member, you might want to introduce them to someone. Here's how you can introduce another person in Afrikaans:

- **Dit is my vriend [name]** (pronounced: dit is may freend [name]) – This means "This is my friend [name]."

For example, if your friend's name is Alex, you would say:

- **Dit is my vriend Alex** (pronounced: dit is may freend alex)

If you are introducing a female friend, you can use the word **vriendin** (pronounced: freen-din), which means "female friend." So, you could say:

- **Dit is my vriendin [name]** (pronounced: dit is may freen-din [name]) – "This is my female friend [name]."

If you want to introduce someone in your family, you can use words like **broer** (pronounced: broor), which means "brother," or **suster** (pronounced: sus-ter), which means "sister." Here are some examples:

- **Dit is my broer** (pronounced: dit is may broor) – "This is my brother."
- **Dit is my suster** (pronounced: dit is may sus-ter) – "This is my sister."

## Polite Introductions

When introducing yourself or others, it's always nice to be polite. You can use the following phrases to make your introduction friendlier:

- **Aangename kennis** (pronounced: ahn-ghah-nah-muh keh-nis) – This means "Nice to meet you."
- **Baie plesier** (pronounced: bah-yuh pleh-seer) – This means "It's a pleasure."

These phrases are good to use when meeting someone for the first time. For example, after you introduce yourself or someone else, you can say **Aangename kennis** to show that you're happy to meet them.

## Talking About Family Members

When introducing your family members, you can use simple phrases like these:

- **Dit is my ma** (pronounced: dit is may mah) – This means "This is my mom."
- **Dit is my pa** (pronounced: dit is may pah) – This means "This is my dad."
- **Dit is my ouma** (pronounced: dit is may oh-mah) – This means "This is my grandmother."
- **Dit is my oupa** (pronounced: dit is may oh-pah) – This means "This is my grandfather."

These phrases are simple ways to introduce members of your family when you meet new people.

## Asking Someone's Name

If you want to ask someone what their name is, you can use this question:

- **Wat is jou naam?** (pronounced: vaht is yow nahm?) – This means "What is your name?"

Here's how to ask someone where they're from:

- **Waar kom jy vandaan?** (pronounced: vahr kom yay fahn-dahn?) – This means "Where are you from?"

These questions are polite ways to get to know someone better when you meet them for the first time.

## Simple Conversations Using Introductions

Here's an example of a simple conversation where two people introduce themselves:

- **Person 1:** Ek is Sarah. (I am Sarah.)
- **Person 2:** Ek is John. Aangename kennis. (I am John. Nice to meet you.)
- **Person 1:** Aangename kennis. Waar kom jy vandaan? (Nice to meet you. Where are you from?)
- **Person 2:** Ek kom van New York. (I am from New York.)

In this conversation, both people introduce themselves, and they ask where the other person is from. You can use conversations like this to practice your introductions in Afrikaans.

## Key Points to Remember

- **Introducing Yourself**: Use **Ek is [your name]** to introduce yourself, like **Ek is Sarah** (I am Sarah).

- **Where You're From**: Use **Ek kom van [place]** to say where you're from, like **Ek kom van New York** (I am from New York).

- **Introducing Someone Else**: Say **Dit is my vriend** (This is my friend) or **Dit is my suster** (This is my sister).

- **Polite Introductions**: Use **Aangename kennis** to say "Nice to meet you" when you meet someone for the first time.

- **Asking for Names**: Ask **Wat is jou naam?** to find out someone's name (What is your name?).

# Chapter 10

# Essential Verbs: Common Actions

Verbs are the action words in a sentence—they tell us what is happening. In Afrikaans, just like in English, verbs are important because they help us talk about what people are doing. In this chapter, we'll look at some essential verbs that describe common actions. These are the words you'll use every day when speaking Afrikaans. By learning these verbs, you'll be able to create simple sentences and talk about everyday activities.

## What are Verbs?

A verb is a word that describes an action, such as "run," "eat," or "play." In Afrikaans, verbs work in a similar way to English. They are used to describe what the subject (the person or thing) is doing. Here are some examples of verbs in Afrikaans:

- **eet** (pronounced: eet) – This means "eat."

- **drink** (pronounced: drink) – This means "drink."

- **swem** (pronounced: swim) – This means "swim."

- **speel** (pronounced: speel) – This means "play."

Each of these verbs describes a common action, and you'll use them often when speaking Afrikaans.

## Common Verbs for Everyday Actions

Let's start by learning some common verbs that describe everyday actions. These are words you can use to talk about what you do, like eating, drinking, reading, and more.

- **eet** (pronounced: eet) – This means "eat." For example, **Ek eet kos** (pronounced: ek eet kaws) means "I eat food."

- **drink** (pronounced: drink) – This means "drink." For example, **Hy drink**

**water** (pronounced: hay drink vah-ter) means "He drinks water."

- **lees** (pronounced: lees) – This means "read." For example, **Sy lees 'n boek** (pronounced: say lees en book) means "She reads a book."

- **skryf** (pronounced: skrayf) – This means "write." For example, **Ek skryf 'n brief** (pronounced: ek skrayf en bree-f) means "I write a letter."

- **speel** (pronounced: speel) – This means "play." For example, **Ons speel sokker** (pronounced: ohns speel soh-ker) means "We play soccer."

- **swem** (pronounced: swim) – This means "swim." For example, **Hulle swem in die see** (pronounced: huh-luh swim in dee say) means "They swim in the sea."

- **loop** (pronounced: lohp) – This means "walk." For example, **Ek loop na skool** (pronounced: ek lohp nah skool) means "I walk to school."

These are some of the most common verbs in Afrikaans, and you can use them in many different sentences to describe what you or someone else is doing.

## Talking About Daily Routines

With these verbs, you can also talk about your daily routine. For example, you can describe what you do each day by using the following phrases:

- **Ek eet ontbyt** (pronounced: ek eet on-bayt) – This means "I eat breakfast."

- **Ek gaan skool toe** (pronounced: ek khahn skool too) – This means "I go to school."

- **Ek speel met my vriende** (pronounced: ek speel met may freen-duh) – This means "I play with my friends."

- **Ek lees 'n boek** (pronounced: ek lees en book) – This means "I read a book."

- **Ek gaan slaap** (pronounced: ek khahn slahp) – This means "I go to sleep."

Notice how each sentence starts with the subject **Ek** (which means "I"), followed by a verb (like **eet** or **gaan**), and then the rest of the sentence. These sentences help you describe what you do throughout the day.

## Verbs for Movement

There are also many verbs in Afrikaans that describe movement. These verbs are useful for talking about where you're going or how you're getting there. Here are some common verbs for movement:

- **loop** (pronounced: lohp) – This means "walk."
- **hardloop** (pronounced: hart-lohp) – This means "run."
- **ry** (pronounced: ray) – This means "ride" or "drive."
- **spring** (pronounced: spring) – This means "jump."
- **vlieg** (pronounced: fleeg) – This means "fly."

For example, you could say:

- **Ek loop huis toe** (pronounced: ek lohp hays too) – This means "I walk home."
- **Sy hardloop vinnig** (pronounced: say hart-lohp fin-nikh) – This means "She runs fast."

These movement verbs will help you talk about how you get from place to place.

## Verbs for Communication

Another important group of verbs are those used for communication. These verbs describe how we talk to each other and share information. Here are some common communication verbs in Afrikaans:

- **praat** (pronounced: praht) – This means "talk" or "speak."
- **luister** (pronounced: loy-ster) – This means "listen."
- **vra** (pronounced: frah) – This means "ask."
- **antwoord** (pronounced: ahnt-voort) – This means "answer."
- **vertel** (pronounced: fer-tel) – This means "tell."

Here are some example sentences using these communication verbs:

- **Ek praat met my ma** (pronounced: ek praht met may mah) – This means "I talk to my mom."

- **Hulle luister na musiek** (pronounced: huh-luh loy-ster nah moo-seek) – This means "They listen to music."

- **Ek vra 'n vraag** (pronounced: ek frah en frahkh) – This means "I ask a question."

These verbs will help you describe how you communicate with others, whether you're asking a question or listening to someone speak.

## Verbs for Thinking and Feeling

In Afrikaans, there are also verbs that describe what you are thinking or feeling. These verbs help you talk about your emotions, thoughts, and opinions. Here are some examples:

- **dink** (pronounced: dink) – This means "think."

- **voel** (pronounced: fool) – This means "feel."

- **liefhê** (pronounced: leef-heh) – This means "love."

- **haat** (pronounced: haht) – This means "hate."

- **hou van** (pronounced: hoh fahn) – This means "like."

Here's how you can use these verbs in sentences:

- **Ek dink aan my werk** (pronounced: ek dink ahn may verk) – This means "I think about my work."

- **Sy voel gelukkig** (pronounced: say fool khe-lukh-ig) – This means "She feels happy."

- **Ek hou van kos** (pronounced: ek hoh fahn k aws) – This means "I like food."

These verbs are important for talking about your emotions and thoughts in Afrikaans.

## Key Points to Remember

- **Common Verbs**: Learn verbs like **eet** (eat), **drink** (drink), and **lees** (read) to talk about everyday actions.

- **Movement Verbs**: Use verbs like **loop** (walk) and **hardloop** (run) to talk about moving from place to place.

- **Communication Verbs**: Learn verbs like **praat** (talk), **luister** (listen), and **vra** (ask) for communication.

- **Thinking and Feeling**: Use verbs like **dink** (think), **voel** (feel), and **liefhê** (love) to talk about thoughts and emotions.

- **Daily Routine Verbs**: Use verbs like **speel** (play), **swem** (swim), and **skryf** (write) to describe your daily activities.

# Chapter 11

# Using Articles: Definite and Indefinite

In every language, we use little words called articles to talk about specific or general things. In English, the words **the**, **a**, and **an** are examples of articles. In Afrikaans, we also have articles, and they work in a similar way. In this chapter, we'll learn how to use the definite and indefinite articles in Afrikaans, and how to tell the difference between them.

## What is an Article?

An article is a word that tells us if we're talking about something specific or something general. In English, **the** is a definite article, which means we are talking about a specific thing. For example, when we say "the book," we are talking about a particular book. On the other hand, **a** or **an** are indefinite articles, which mean we are talking about something more general. For example, when we say "a book," we could be talking about any book, not a specific one.

In Afrikaans, there are two main articles: **die** (pronounced: dee), which is the definite article, and **'n** (pronounced: uh), which is the indefinite article.

## The Definite Article: "Die"

The definite article in Afrikaans is **die**, and it works just like the word "the" in English. We use it when we're talking about a specific person, place, or thing. Here are some examples:

- **die boek** (pronounced: dee book) – This means "the book." We are talking about one particular book.

- **die kat** (pronounced: dee kaht) – This means "the cat." We are talking about a specific cat.

# USING ARTICLES: DEFINITE AND INDEFINITE

- **die huis** (pronounced: dee hays) – This means "the house." We are talking about a particular house.

Just like in English, we use **die** when we want to refer to a specific thing that both the speaker and the listener know about. For example, if you and your friend are looking at the same book, you would say:

- **Dit is die boek** (pronounced: dit is dee book) – This means "This is the book."

Here, you are talking about a specific book that you both can see.

## The Indefinite Article: "'n"

The indefinite article in Afrikaans is **'n** (pronounced: uh), and it works like the words "a" or "an" in English. We use it when we are talking about something general, not a specific thing. Here are some examples:

- **'n boek** (pronounced: uh book) – This means "a book." We are not talking about any specific book.

- **'n hond** (pronounced: uh hont) – This means "a dog." We are talking about any dog, not a particular one.

- **'n huis** (pronounced: uh hays) – This means "a house." It could be any house, not a specific one.

We use **'n** when we're talking about something general, something that hasn't been mentioned before, or something that the listener doesn't know about yet. For example, if you are talking to someone about a new book, you would say:

- **Ek het 'n boek** (pronounced: ek het uh book) – This means "I have a book."

In this case, the person you are speaking to doesn't know which book you are talking about because you haven't mentioned it yet.

## Using Articles in Sentences

Now that we know the difference between **die** (the) and **'n** (a), let's look at how we can use them in sentences. Here are a few examples:

- **Ek lees die boek** (pronounced: ek lees dee book) – This means "I am reading the book." In this sentence, you are talking about a specific book.

- **Sy het 'n hond** (pronounced: say het uh hont) – This means "She has a dog." In this sentence, we are talking about any dog, not a specific one.

- **Ons eet die kos** (pronounced: ohns eet dee kaws) – This means "We are eating the food." Here, **die** tells us that we are talking about specific food, not just any food.

- **Hy koop 'n kar** (pronounced: hay koop uh kar) – This means "He is buying a car." We don't know which car, it could be any car.

As you can see, **die** is used when we are talking about something specific, and **'n** is used when we are talking about something more general or unknown.

## Articles and Plural Nouns

In Afrikaans, articles work the same way whether the noun is singular (one thing) or plural (more than one thing). For example, let's look at how we use **die** and **'n** with both singular and plural nouns:

- **Die hond** (pronounced: dee hont) – This means "The dog" (one dog).

- **Die honde** (pronounced: dee hon-duh) – This means "The dogs" (more than one dog).

- **'n hond** (pronounced: uh hont) – This means "A dog" (one dog).

- **'n paar honde** (pronounced: uh pahr hon-duh) – This means "A few dogs" (more than one dog).

Notice that the article **die** stays the same whether the noun is singular or plural. The same is true for the indefinite article **'n**. The noun changes to show whether we are talking about one thing or many, but the article stays the same.

## Important Note: Capitalization of "'n"

One thing to remember when using the indefinite article **'n** is that it is never capitalized, even at the beginning of a sentence. Here's an example:

- **'n Hond is my gunsteling troeteldier** (pronounced: uh hont is may khun-ste-ling truh-tel-deer) – This means "A dog is my favorite pet."

Even though **'n** is at the beginning of the sentence, it is still written with a lowercase letter. In this case, the word following **'n**, such as **Hond**, will start with a capital letter if it is the first word in the sentence.

## Summary of Using Articles

To sum up, the article **die** is used to talk about specific things, while **'n** is used to talk about general or non-specific things. Both articles are important for building clear and correct sentences in Afrikaans.

## Key Points to Remember

- **Die for Definite Things**: Use **die** to talk about specific things, like **die boek** (the book).

- **'n for Indefinite Things**: Use **'n** to talk about general things, like **'n hond** (a dog).

- **Articles with Plurals**: **Die** and **'n** are used the same way with both singular and plural nouns, like **die honde** (the dogs).

- **Never Capitalize "'n"**: The article **'n** is never capitalized, even at the start of a sentence.

- **Use Articles in Everyday Speech**: Practice using **die** and **'n** in sentences to describe specific and general things.

# Chapter 12

# Nouns: People, Places, and Things

Nouns are one of the most important parts of any language because they allow us to talk about people, places, and things. In Afrikaans, nouns work similarly to how they do in English, and learning them will help you describe the world around you. In this chapter, we'll learn about nouns and how they are used in Afrikaans, with lots of examples to help you get started.

## What is a Noun?

A noun is a word that names a person, place, or thing. Nouns help us identify the things we see, hear, and experience. In Afrikaans, just like in English, nouns are divided into three main categories: people, places, and things. Let's go through each category and learn some examples.

## Nouns for People

Nouns that name people are some of the most common words you'll use. These can be words for family members, friends, or jobs. Here are some examples of nouns that describe people in Afrikaans:

- **man** (pronounced: mahn) – This means "man."

- **vrou** (pronounced: froh) – This means "woman."

- **seun** (pronounced: say-un) – This means "boy."

- **meisie** (pronounced: may-see) – This means "girl."

- **vriende** (pronounced: freen-duh) – This means "friends."

- **onderwyser** (pronounced: on-der-vay-ser) – This means "teacher."

- **dokter** (pronounced: dok-ter) – This means "doctor."

These nouns help you talk about the people in your life. For example, you might say:

- **Ek is 'n meisie** (pronounced: ek is uh may-see) – This means "I am a girl."

- **Hy is 'n onderwyser** (pronounced: hay is uh on-der-vay-ser) – This means "He is a teacher."

Notice how these nouns are used with articles like **'n** (a) or **die** (the) depending on whether you're talking about something general or specific.

## Nouns for Places

Now let's look at nouns that name places. These are words for different locations, whether they are cities, countries, or everyday places like the park or school. Here are some examples of place nouns in Afrikaans:

- **huis** (pronounced: hays) – This means "house" or "home."

- **skool** (pronounced: skool) – This means "school."

- **stad** (pronounced: staht) – This means "city."

- **winkel** (pronounced: vink-el) – This means "store" or "shop."

- **park** (pronounced: park) – This means "park."

- **strand** (pronounced: strahnt) – This means "beach."

- **land** (pronounced: lahnt) – This means "country."

These place nouns help you talk about where you are or where something happens. For example, you might say:

- **Ek gaan skool toe** (pronounced: ek khahn skool too) – This means "I am going to school."

- **Ons gaan na die park** (pronounced: ohns khahn nah dee park) – This means "We are going to the park."

As you can see, these nouns are essential for talking about places you visit or live in.

## Nouns for Things

Nouns that describe things are used to talk about objects around you, like books, food, or toys. Here are some examples of nouns for things in Afrikaans:

- **boek** (pronounced: book) – This means "book."
- **kos** (pronounced: kaws) – This means "food."
- **bal** (pronounced: bahl) – This means "ball."
- **stoel** (pronounced: stool) – This means "chair."
- **motor** (pronounced: moh-ter) – This means "car."
- **rekenaar** (pronounced: ray-kuh-nahr) – This means "computer."

Here are some example sentences using these nouns:

- **Ek lees 'n boek** (pronounced: ek lees uh book) – This means "I am reading a book."
- **Hy speel met die bal** (pronounced: hay speel met dee bahl) – This means "He is playing with the ball."

Nouns for things are some of the most common words you'll use in Afrikaans because they help you talk about everyday objects.

## Singular and Plural Nouns

In Afrikaans, nouns can be either singular (one person, place, or thing) or plural (more than one person, place, or thing). Just like in English, we change the word to show whether we're talking about one thing or many. Here are some examples:

- **boek** (pronounced: book) – This means "book" (one book).
- **boeke** (pronounced: book-uh) – This means "books" (more than one book).
- **huis** (pronounced: hays) – This means "house" (one house).
- **huise** (pronounced: hays-uh) – This means "houses" (more than one house).

Notice that for most nouns, you add **-e** to make the noun plural. Here are a few more examples:

- **stoel** (pronounced: stool) – This means "chair" (one chair).

- **stoele** (pronounced: stool-uh) – This means "chairs" (more than one chair).

Learning how to form plurals will help you talk about more than one person, place, or thing at a time.

## Proper Nouns vs. Common Nouns

Nouns in Afrikaans can also be divided into two types: proper nouns and common nouns. Let's look at the difference:

- **Proper nouns** are names of specific people, places, or things. These are names like **John** (pronounced: john), **Kaapstad** (pronounced: kahp-staht) for "Cape Town," or **Google** (pronounced: goo-gel).

- **Common nouns** are general words for people, places, or things, like **man** (man), **stad** (city), or **boek** (book).

Proper nouns always start with a capital letter in both English and Afrikaans, while common nouns do not.

## Using Nouns in Sentences

Now that you know what nouns are and how to use them, let's look at how they fit into sentences. In Afrikaans, nouns usually come after articles like **'n** (a) or **die** (the). For example:

- **Dit is 'n boek** (pronounced: dit is uh book) – This means "This is a book."

- **Dit is die boek** (pronounced: dit is dee book) – This means "This is the book."

As you can see, nouns are an important part of every sentence, and they help describe who or what the sentence is about.

## Key Points to Remember

- **Nouns Describe People, Places, and Things**: Nouns help us talk about people, like **seun** (boy), places like **skool** (school), and things like **boek** (book).

- **Singular and Plural Nouns:** Singular nouns describe one thing, like **boek** (book), while plural nouns describe more than one, like **boeke** (books).

- **Proper and Common Nouns:** Proper nouns, like **Kaapstad** (Cape Town), are names of specific people or places, while common nouns, like **stad** (city), are general.

- **Articles with Nouns:** Nouns are often used with articles like **'n** (a) or **die** (the), as in **'n huis** (a house) or **die huis** (the house).

- **Nouns in Everyday Use:** You will use nouns in nearly every sentence to talk about the people, places, and things around you.

# Chapter 13

# Adjectives: Describing People and Things

Adjectives are words that help us describe people, places, and things. In Afrikaans, just like in English, adjectives make our sentences more interesting by telling us more about nouns. They help answer questions like "What kind?" or "How many?" In this chapter, we will learn about how to use adjectives in Afrikaans, how they work with nouns, and how to make sentences more descriptive and fun!

## What is an Adjective?

An adjective is a word that describes or gives more information about a noun (a person, place, or thing). Adjectives can describe how something looks, feels, or behaves. For example, in the sentence "The cat is soft," the word **soft** is an adjective because it describes the cat.

In Afrikaans, adjectives work the same way. Here are a few examples of adjectives in Afrikaans:

- **mooi** (pronounced: moy) – This means "beautiful" or "pretty."

- **groot** (pronounced: khroot) – This means "big."

- **vinnig** (pronounced: fin-nikh) – This means "fast."

- **lekker** (pronounced: lek-er) – This means "tasty" or "nice."

- **oud** (pronounced: owt) – This means "old."

- **jonk** (pronounced: yonk) – This means "young."

These words describe different qualities of people or things. Let's look at how to use them in sentences.

## Using Adjectives with Nouns

In Afrikaans, adjectives usually come before the noun they describe, just like in English. Let's look at a few examples:

- **'n Groot huis** (pronounced: uh khroot hays) – This means "a big house."

- **'n Vinnige kar** (pronounced: uh fin-nikh-e kar) – This means "a fast car."

- **'n Mooi blom** (pronounced: uh moy blom) – This means "a beautiful flower."

In these examples, the adjectives **groot** (big), **vinnige** (fast), and **mooi** (beautiful) come before the nouns **huis** (house), **kar** (car), and **blom** (flower) to describe them. This is how adjectives are usually used in sentences to give more information about the noun.

## Describing People

Adjectives are very useful when talking about people. You can use them to describe how someone looks or acts. Here are some common adjectives used to describe people in Afrikaans:

- **slim** (pronounced: slim) – This means "smart."

- **vriendelik** (pronounced: freen-de-likh) – This means "friendly."

- **snaaks** (pronounced: snaaks) – This means "funny."

- **moeg** (pronounced: moog) – This means "tired."

- **gelukkig** (pronounced: khe-lukh-ig) – This means "happy."

Here are some examples of these adjectives used in sentences:

- **Sy is slim** (pronounced: say is slim) – This means "She is smart."

- **Hy is vriendelik** (pronounced: hay is freen-de-likh) – This means "He is friendly."

- **Ek is moeg** (pronounced: ek is moog) – This means "I am tired."

These adjectives help describe how people feel or behave. They can be used in many different sentences to talk about the people around you.

# ADJECTIVES: DESCRIBING PEOPLE AND THINGS

## Describing Things

Adjectives are also important when talking about things. They help you describe objects, animals, or places. Here are some adjectives you can use to describe things in Afrikaans:

- **skoon** (pronounced: skoon) – This means "clean."

- **warm** (pronounced: varrm) – This means "warm."

- **sag** (pronounced: sakh) – This means "soft."

- **hard** (pronounced: haart) – This means "hard."

- **lelik** (pronounced: lay-likh) – This means "ugly."

Let's look at some examples of these adjectives in sentences:

- **Die water is warm** (pronounced: dee vah-ter is varrm) – This means "The water is warm."

- **Ek het 'n sag kussing** (pronounced: ek het uh sakh koo-sing) – This means "I have a soft pillow."

- **Die boek is lelik** (pronounced: dee book is lay-likh) – This means "The book is ugly."

As you can see, adjectives help describe the qualities of objects or things, making your sentences more interesting and detailed.

## Making Comparisons with Adjectives

Sometimes, you want to compare two things and say that one is bigger, smaller, or better than the other. In Afrikaans, you can use adjectives to make comparisons. Here's how you do it:

- **groot** (big) – **groter** (bigger)

- **vinnig** (fast) – **vinniger** (faster)

- **mooi** (pretty) – **mooier** (prettier)

To compare two things, you add **-er** to the adjective. Here are some examples:

- **Die huis is groter as die motor** (pronounced: dee hays is khroot-er ahs dee moh-ter) – This means "The house is bigger than the car."

- **Hy is vinniger as sy broer** (pronounced: hay is fin-nikh-er ahs say broor) – This means "He is faster than his brother."

Notice how the word **as** (pronounced: ahs), which means "than," is used when comparing two things. This structure helps you describe how one thing is different from another.

## Superlative Adjectives

If you want to say something is the biggest, best, or fastest of all, you can use superlative adjectives. In Afrikaans, we add **-ste** to the adjective to form the superlative. For example:

- **groot** (big) – **grootste** (biggest)
- **vinnig** (fast) – **vinnigste** (fastest)
- **mooi** (pretty) – **mooiste** (prettiest)

Here are some examples in sentences:

- **Dit is die grootste huis** (pronounced: dit is dee khroot-ste hays) – This means "This is the biggest house."
- **Hy is die vinnigste kind** (pronounced: hay is dee fin-nikh-ste kint) – This means "He is the fastest child."

Superlative adjectives help you describe the most or least of something, which is useful when making comparisons in Afrikaans.

## Key Points to Remember

- **Adjectives Describe Nouns**: Adjectives give more information about people, places, and things, like **groot** (big) or **mooi** (beautiful).
- **Adjectives Come Before Nouns**: In Afrikaans, adjectives usually come before the noun they describe, like **'n groot huis** (a big house).
- **Comparative Adjectives**: Add **-er** to the adjective to compare two things, like **groter** (bigger).
- **Superlative Adjectives**: Add **-ste** to say something is the most, like **grootste** (biggest).
- **Adjectives Describe People and Things**: Use adjectives to describe how people feel

or what things look like, such as **vriendelik** (friendly) or **skoon** (clean).

# Chapter 14

# Forming Questions in Afrikaans

In any language, asking questions is one of the most important skills to have. In Afrikaans, forming questions is quite simple, and it often follows similar patterns to English. Whether you want to ask someone's name, find out the time, or ask where they are from, this chapter will show you how to form different kinds of questions in Afrikaans.

## Basic Yes/No Questions

In Afrikaans, forming a yes/no question is easy. You usually just change the word order by placing the verb (the action word) before the subject (the person or thing doing the action). Let's look at some examples:

- **Hy eet** (pronounced: hay eet) – This means "He eats."
- **Eet hy?** (pronounced: eet hay) – This means "Does he eat?"

Notice that in the statement "Hy eet," the verb **eet** (eat) comes after the subject **hy** (he). In the question "Eet hy?" the verb **eet** comes before the subject **hy**. This is the basic way to form yes/no questions in Afrikaans.

Here are more examples of yes/no questions:

- **Sy speel** (pronounced: say speel) – This means "She plays."
- **Speel sy?** (pronounced: speel say) – This means "Does she play?"
- **Jy lees** (pronounced: yay lees) – This means "You read."
- **Lees jy?** (pronounced: lees yay) – This means "Do you read?"

As you can see, asking a yes/no question is as simple as swapping the verb and subject.

## Question Words in Afrikaans

Sometimes, you want to ask a more specific question, like "What is your name?" or "Where are you from?" In Afrikaans, there are special question words to help you ask these kinds of questions. Here are some of the most common question words:

- **Wat** (pronounced: vaht) – This means "What."

- **Waar** (pronounced: vahr) – This means "Where."

- **Wie** (pronounced: vee) – This means "Who."

- **Waarom** (pronounced: vahr-om) – This means "Why."

- **Hoe** (pronounced: hoo) – This means "How."

- **Wanneer** (pronounced: vah-neer) – This means "When."

These question words are used at the beginning of a question, and they help you get more information than just a yes or no answer. Let's look at some examples:

- **Wat is jou naam?** (pronounced: vaht is yow nahm) – This means "What is your name?"

- **Waar woon jy?** (pronounced: vahr voon yay) – This means "Where do you live?"

- **Wie is hy?** (pronounced: vee is hay) – This means "Who is he?"

- **Waarom huil sy?** (pronounced: vahr-om hayl say) – This means "Why is she crying?"

- **Hoe gaan dit met jou?** (pronounced: hoo khahn dit met yow) – This means "How are you?"

- **Wanneer kom hy?** (pronounced: vah-neer khom hay) – This means "When is he coming?"

These question words help you ask for specific information and can be used in many different situations.

## Using "Is" in Questions

Just like in English, you can use the verb "is" in Afrikaans to form questions. Here's how:

- **Hy is moeg** (pronounced: hay is moog) – This means "He is tired."

- **Is hy moeg?** (pronounced: is hay moog) – This means "Is he tired?"

Notice that just like with yes/no questions, the verb **is** is moved to the front of the sentence when you are asking a question.

Here are more examples:

- **Sy is gelukkig** (pronounced: say is khe-lukh-ig) – This means "She is happy."
- **Is sy gelukkig?** (pronounced: is say khe-lukh-ig) – This means "Is she happy?"

Asking questions with "is" is simple, and you just need to switch the word order to form the question.

## Asking About Possession

If you want to ask if someone has something or who something belongs to, you can use the verb **het** (have). Here's how you can form questions about possession:

- **Jy het 'n boek** (pronounced: yay het uh book) – This means "You have a book."
- **Het jy 'n boek?** (pronounced: het yay uh book) – This means "Do you have a book?"

Once again, notice how the verb **het** is moved to the front to ask the question. You can also ask questions like "Whose is this?" in Afrikaans using the word **wie se** (whose):

- **Wie se boek is dit?** (pronounced: vee suh book is dit) – This means "Whose book is this?"

## Questions with "Can" and "May"

If you want to ask if someone is able to do something or if they are allowed to do something, you can use the verbs **kan** (can) or **mag** (may). Let's look at some examples:

- **Jy kan dans** (pronounced: yay khan dahns) – This means "You can dance."
- **Kan jy dans?** (pronounced: khan yay dahns) – This means "Can you dance?"

Here's another example with the word **mag**:

- **Jy mag speel** (pronounced: yay makh speel) – This means "You may play."
- **Mag jy speel?** (pronounced: makh yay speel) – This means "May you play?"

These questions are useful for asking about ability or permission.

## Forming Negative Questions

In Afrikaans, you can also ask negative questions, which are questions that use the word **nie** (not). Here's how you can do that:

- **Jy lees nie** (pronounced: yay lees nee) – This means "You do not read."

- **Lees jy nie?** (pronounced: lees yay nee) – This means "Don't you read?"

To form a negative question, you just add **nie** after the verb or at the end of the sentence. Let's look at another example:

- **Sy speel nie** (pronounced: say speel nee) – This means "She does not play."

- **Speel sy nie?** (pronounced: speel say nee) – This means "Doesn't she play?"

## Key Points to Remember

- **Yes/No Questions**: To form yes/no questions, move the verb before the subject, like **Eet jy?** (Do you eat?).

- **Question Words**: Use question words like **Wat** (What) or **Waar** (Where) to ask for specific information, like **Wat is jou naam?** (What is your name?).

- **Using "Is" in Questions**: Swap the verb **is** to the front to ask questions, like **Is hy moeg?** (Is he tired?).

- **Asking About Possession**: Use **het** (have) to ask about possession, like **Het jy 'n boek?** (Do you have a book?).

- **Negative Questions**: Add **nie** to ask negative questions, like **Lees jy nie?** (Don't you read?).

# Chapter 15

# Basic Conversation Skills: Asking and Answering

One of the most important parts of learning a new language is being able to have simple conversations. In Afrikaans, you can easily ask and answer basic questions, which will help you talk to people and understand them better. In this chapter, we'll learn how to ask and answer common questions, introduce yourself, and talk about everyday things. By the end, you'll be able to start a basic conversation in Afrikaans!

## Introducing Yourself

The first step in any conversation is introducing yourself. In Afrikaans, you can do this with a few simple phrases. Let's start with how to say your name:

- **Ek is [jou naam]** (pronounced: ek is [yow nahm]) – This means "I am [your name]."

If you want to ask someone else's name, you can use this question:

- **Wat is jou naam?** (pronounced: vaht is yow nahm) – This means "What is your name?"

So, if someone asks you this question, you can respond with **Ek is [jou naam]**. For example:

- **Wat is jou naam?**

- **Ek is Sarah** (pronounced: ek is sah-rah) – This means "I am Sarah."

This is a simple and friendly way to start a conversation.

## Asking About Someone's Well-Being

After introducing yourself, it's polite to ask someone how they are doing. In Afrikaans, you can use the phrase:

# BASIC CONVERSATION SKILLS: ASKING AND ANSWERING

- **Hoe gaan dit met jou?** (pronounced: hoo khahn dit met yow) – This means "How are you?"

If someone asks you this, here are some ways you can respond:

- **Dit gaan goed, dankie** (pronounced: dit khahn khoot, dahn-kee) – This means "I'm fine, thank you."
- **Ek is moeg** (pronounced: ek is moog) – This means "I am tired."
- **Ek is gelukkig** (pronounced: ek is khe-lukh-ig) – This means "I am happy."

Asking someone how they are and responding to that question is a great way to keep the conversation going.

## Talking About Where You're From

Another common question in conversations is asking where someone is from. In Afrikaans, you can ask:

- **Waar kom jy vandaan?** (pronounced: vahr khom yay fahn-dahn) – This means "Where are you from?"

If someone asks you this question, here's how you can answer:

- **Ek kom van [plek]** (pronounced: ek khom fahn [place]) – This means "I am from [place]."

For example:

- **Ek kom van New York** (pronounced: ek khom fahn new york) – This means "I am from New York."

Talking about where you're from helps the other person get to know you better.

## Asking About Age

If you want to ask someone how old they are, you can use this question:

- **Hoe oud is jy?** (pronounced: hoo owt is yay) – This means "How old are you?"

To answer, you can say:

- **Ek is [ouderdom] jaar oud** (pronounced: ek is [age] yah-r owt) – This means "I am

[age] years old."

For example:

- **Ek is 12 jaar oud** (pronounced: ek is twahlf yah-r owt) – This means "I am 12 years old."

Asking and answering questions about age is another simple way to have a conversation.

## Talking About Your Day

You might also want to talk about what you're doing or how your day is going. In Afrikaans, you can ask:

- **Wat doen jy?** (pronounced: vaht doohn yay) – This means "What are you doing?"

To answer, you can say:

- **Ek lees** (pronounced: ek lees) – This means "I am reading."
- **Ek speel buite** (pronounced: ek speel bay-tuh) – This means "I am playing outside."
- **Ek kyk televisie** (pronounced: ek kayk tell-eh-vee-see) – This means "I am watching television."

Asking someone what they are doing helps you talk about your day and share your activities with each other.

## Talking About Favorites

Another fun way to keep a conversation going is to talk about your favorite things. In Afrikaans, you can ask:

- **Wat is jou gunsteling [iets]?** (pronounced: vaht is yow khun-ste-ling [something]) – This means "What is your favorite [something]?"

For example, you can ask about someone's favorite color:

- **Wat is jou gunsteling kleur?** (pronounced: vaht is yow khun-ste-ling kleer) – This means "What is your favorite color?"

To answer, you can say:

- **My gunsteling kleur is blou** (pronounced: may khun-ste-ling kleer is blow) – This means "My favorite color is blue."

Here are some more examples:

- **Wat is jou gunsteling kos?** (pronounced: vaht is yow khun-ste-ling kaws) – This means "What is your favorite food?"

- **Wat is jou gunsteling dier?** (pronounced: vaht is yow khun-ste-ling deer) – This means "What is your favorite animal?"

Talking about your favorite things is a fun way to share more about yourself and learn more about others.

## Responding to Yes/No Questions

Sometimes, the questions you ask in a conversation only need a yes or no answer. Let's learn how to answer yes/no questions in Afrikaans:

- **Ja** (pronounced: yah) – This means "Yes."

- **Nee** (pronounced: nee) – This means "No."

Here are some examples of yes/no questions and how to answer them:

- **Kan jy sokker speel?** (pronounced: khan yay soh-ker speel) – This means "Can you play soccer?"

- **Ja, ek kan** (pronounced: yah, ek khan) – This means "Yes, I can."

- **Nee, ek kan nie** (pronounced: nee, ek khan nee) – This means "No, I can't."

Here's another example:

- **Lees jy 'n boek?** (pronounced: lees yay uh book) – This means "Are you reading a book?"

- **Ja, ek lees 'n boek** (pronounced: yah, ek lees uh book) – This means "Yes, I am reading a book."

- **Nee, ek lees nie** (pronounced: nee, ek lees nee) – This means "No, I am not reading."

Knowing how to answer yes/no questions will make your conversations flow more easily.

## Common Polite Phrases

In any conversation, it's important to be polite. Here are some useful phrases to help you sound polite in Afrikaans:

- **Dankie** (pronounced: dahn-kee) – This means "Thank you."

- **Asseblief (pronounced: ah-suh-bleef) – This means "Please."**

- **Verskoon my (pronounced: fer-skohn may) – This means "Excuse me."**

- **Dit is lekker om jou te ontmoet (pronounced: dit is lek-er om yow tuh on-moet)** – This means "It's nice to meet you."

**Using these phrases will help you show good manners and respect when talking to others.**

## Key Points to Remember

- **Introducing Yourself:** Use **Ek** is [your name] to introduce yourself, and ask **Wat is jou naam?** to ask someone's name.

- **Asking How Someone Is:** Ask **Hoe gaan dit met jou?** (How are you?) to check on someone's well-being, and respond with phrases like **Dit gaan goed, dankie** (I'm fine, thank you).

- **Talking About Favorites:** Use **Wat is jou gunsteling [iets]?** (What is your favorite [something]?) to talk about favorite things.

- **Responding to Yes/No Questions:** Use **Ja** (Yes) or **Nee** (No) to answer yes/no questions.

- **Polite Phrases:** Use words like **Dankie** (Thank you) and **Asseblief** (Please) to be polite in conversations.

# Chapter 16

# Possessive Pronouns: Mine, Yours, Ours

When we talk about things that belong to us or others, we use special words called possessive pronouns. Possessive pronouns help us show ownership, like saying "This is my book" or "That is your toy." In Afrikaans, possessive pronouns work similarly to English, but with a few differences. In this chapter, we'll learn how to use possessive pronouns like "mine," "yours," and "ours" in Afrikaans.

## What Are Possessive Pronouns?

A possessive pronoun is a word that shows who something belongs to. In English, words like **mine**, **yours**, and **ours** are possessive pronouns. They help us talk about ownership. For example, we say "That book is mine" to show that the book belongs to us.

In Afrikaans, possessive pronouns work the same way. Here are the common possessive pronouns in Afrikaans:

- **myne** (pronounced: may-nuh) – This means "mine."
- **joune** (pronounced: yow-nuh) – This means "yours."
- **syne** (pronounced: say-nuh) – This means "his."
- **hare** (pronounced: hah-ruh) – This means "hers."
- **ons s'n** (pronounced: ohns sen) – This means "ours."
- **hulle s'n** (pronounced: huh-luh sen) – This means "theirs."

These pronouns help you talk about who something belongs to. Let's see how to use them in sentences.

## Using "Myne" (Mine)

If something belongs to you, you use the word **myne**, which means "mine." For example, if you're talking about your book, you can say:

- **Die boek is myne** (pronounced: dee book is may-nuh) – This means "The book is mine."

Here's another example:

- **Die pen is myne** (pronounced: dee pen is may-nuh) – This means "The pen is mine."

You can use **myne** for anything that belongs to you, whether it's a book, a toy, or anything else.

## Using "Joune" (Yours)

If something belongs to someone else, you use the word **joune**, which means "yours." Here's an example:

- **Die potlood is joune** (pronounced: dee pot-loht is yow-nuh) – This means "The pencil is yours."

This shows that the pencil belongs to the person you are speaking to. You can also say:

- **Die bal is joune** (pronounced: dee bahl is yow-nuh) – This means "The ball is yours."

**Joune** is useful whenever you want to say that something belongs to someone else.

## Using "Syne" (His) and "Hare" (Hers)

If something belongs to a boy or man, you use the word **syne**, which means "his." For example:

- **Die speelding is syne** (pronounced: dee speel-ding is say-nuh) – This means "The toy is his."

If something belongs to a girl or woman, you use the word **hare**, which means "hers." For example:

- **Die tas is hare** (pronounced: dee tahs is hah-ruh) – This means "The suitcase is hers."

These possessive pronouns are used to show ownership depending on whether the person is male or female.

## Using "Ons s'n" (Ours)

If something belongs to you and others, you use the word **ons s'n**, which means "ours." Here's an example:

- **Die huis is ons s'n** (pronounced: dee hays is ohns sen) – This means "The house is ours."

You can use **ons s'n** when talking about things that belong to a group of people that includes you. Another example is:

- **Die kar is ons s'n** (pronounced: dee kar is ohns sen) – This means "The car is ours."

## Using "Hulle s'n" (Theirs)

If something belongs to a group of people not including you, you use the word **hulle s'n**, which means "theirs." For example:

- **Die honde is hulle s'n** (pronounced: dee hon-duh is huh-luh sen) – This means "The dogs are theirs."

Here's another example:

- **Die fietse is hulle s'n** (pronounced: dee feets-uh is huh-luh sen) – This means "The bikes are theirs."

**Hulle s'n** is used when you're talking about something that belongs to other people.

## Asking About Possession

Sometimes, you may want to ask someone who something belongs to. In Afrikaans, you can ask:

- **Wie se [iets] is dit?** (pronounced: vee suh [iets] is dit) – This means "Whose [something] is this?"

For example:

- **Wie se boek is dit?** (pronounced: vee suh book is dit) – This means "Whose book is this?"

- **Wie se fiets is dit?** (pronounced: vee suh feets is dit) – This means "Whose bike is this?"

To answer these questions, you can use the possessive pronouns we have learned. For example:

- **Dit is myne** (pronounced: dit is may-nuh) – This means "It is mine."

- **Dit is joune** (pronounced: dit is yow-nuh) – This means "It is yours."

- **Dit is syne** (pronounced: dit is say-nuh) – This means "It is his."

- **Dit is hare** (pronounced: dit is hah-ruh) – This means "It is hers."

- **Dit is ons s'n** (pronounced: dit is ohns sen) – This means "It is ours."

- **Dit is hulle s'n** (pronounced: dit is huh-luh sen) – This means "It is theirs."

## Key Points to Remember

- **Myne means mine**: Use **myne** to say something belongs to you, like **Die boek is myne** ("The book is mine").

- **Joune means yours**: Use **joune** to talk about something that belongs to someone else, like **Die bal is joune** ("The ball is yours").

- **Syne and hare**: Use **syne** for "his" and **hare** for "hers," like **Die fiets is syne** ("The bike is his").

- **Ons s'n means ours**: Use **ons s'n** to talk about something that belongs to your group, like **Die huis is ons s'n** ("The house is ours").

- **Hulle s'n means theirs**: Use **hulle s'n** to say something belongs to others, like **Die tasse is hulle s'n** ("The suitcases are theirs").

# Chapter 17

# Family and Relationships Vocabulary

In every language, talking about family and relationships is very important. In Afrikaans, just like in English, there are specific words to describe your family members and the relationships you have with them. In this chapter, we will learn the Afrikaans words for family members, how to describe relationships, and how to use these words in sentences. By the end of this chapter, you'll be able to talk about your family and relationships in Afrikaans!

## Basic Family Members

Let's start by learning the basic words for family members. These are the words you will use most often when talking about your family:

- **ma** (pronounced: mah) – This means "mom" or "mother."

- **pa** (pronounced: pah) – This means "dad" or "father."

- **broer** (pronounced: broor) – This means "brother."

- **suster** (pronounced: sus-ter) – This means "sister."

- **ouma** (pronounced: oh-mah) – This means "grandmother."

- **oupa** (pronounced: oh-pah) – This means "grandfather."

These words are used to describe your immediate family members. Let's see how you can use them in sentences:

- **My ma is baie lief vir my** (pronounced: may mah is bah-ye leef fur may) – This means "My mom loves me very much."

- **Ek het 'n broer en 'n suster** (pronounced: ek het uh broor en uh sus-ter) – This means

"I have a brother and a sister."

Using these words will help you talk about your close family members.

## Extended Family Members

Now let's learn some words for extended family members, like aunts, uncles, and cousins. Here are the Afrikaans words for these family members:

- **oom** (pronounced: ohm) – This means "uncle."
- **tannie** (pronounced: tahn-nee) – This means "aunt."
- **neef** (pronounced: neef) – This means "male cousin."
- **niggie** (pronounced: nik-ee) – This means "female cousin."

Here are some examples of these words in sentences:

- **My oom kom kuier** (pronounced: may ohm khom coy-er) – This means "My uncle is coming to visit."
- **Ek het 'n neef en 'n niggie** (pronounced: ek het uh neef en uh nik-ee) – This means "I have a male cousin and a female cousin."

These words will help you talk about the wider members of your family.

## Talking About Parents and Children

In Afrikaans, there are also words to describe relationships between parents and their children. Here are the common words used for this:

- **ouer** (pronounced: oh-er) – This means "parent."
- **kind** (pronounced: kint) – This means "child."
- **seun** (pronounced: say-un) – This means "son."
- **dogter** (pronounced: dok-ter) – This means "daughter."

Here are some examples of how to use these words in sentences:

- **My ouers is baie goed** (pronounced: may oh-ers is bah-ye khoot) – This means "My parents are very good."

- **Ek het twee kinders** (pronounced: ek het twee kin-ders) – This means "I have two children."

- **Hy is my seun** (pronounced: hay is may say-un) – This means "He is my son."

- **Sy is my dogter** (pronounced: say is may dok-ter) – This means "She is my daughter."

Using these words, you can describe the relationships between parents and their children in Afrikaans.

## Describing Relationships

In addition to knowing the words for family members, it's important to know how to describe relationships between them. Here are some useful phrases:

- **Ek is die kind van my ma en pa** (pronounced: ek is dee kint fahn may mah en pah) – This means "I am the child of my mom and dad."

- **Hulle is my ouers** (pronounced: huh-luh is may oh-ers) – This means "They are my parents."

- **Ons is 'n groot familie** (pronounced: ohns is uh khroot fah-mee-lee) – This means "We are a big family."

- **Sy is my suster en ek is haar broer** (pronounced: say is may sus-ter en ek is hahr broor) – This means "She is my sister and I am her brother."

These phrases will help you explain how people in your family are related to each other.

## Talking About Marriage and Partners

In Afrikaans, there are also words to describe your relationship with your husband or wife. Here are the key words to know:

- **man** (pronounced: mahn) – This means "husband."

- **vrou** (pronounced: froh) – This means "wife."

- **eggenoot** (pronounced: ehkh-gen-oh-t) – This means "spouse" (can be male or female).

Here's how you can use these words in sentences:

- **Sy is my vrou** (pronounced: say is may froh) – This means "She is my wife."

- **Hy is my man** (pronounced: hay is may mahn) – This means "He is my husband."
- **Ek is sy eggenoot** (pronounced: ek is say ehkh-gen-oh-t) – This means "I am his spouse."

These words will help you talk about married relationships and partners.

## Describing In-Laws

Sometimes you need to talk about family members related by marriage. In Afrikaans, here are the words for in-laws:

- **skoonma** (pronounced: skoon-mah) – This means "mother-in-law."
- **skoonpa** (pronounced: skoon-pah) – This means "father-in-law."
- **skoonseun** (pronounced: skoon-say-un) – This means "son-in-law."
- **skoon dogter** (pronounced: skoon dok-ter) – This means "daughter-in-law."

Here's how you can use these words:

- **My skoonma is baie gaaf** (pronounced: may skoon-mah is bah-ye gahf) – This means "My mother-in-law is very kind."
- **Hy is my skoonseun** (pronounced: hay is may skoon-say-un) – This means "He is my son-in-law."

These words help you describe relationships with family members related to you by marriage.

## Key Points to Remember

- **Basic Family Members**: Learn words like **ma** (mom), **pa** (dad), **broer** (brother), and **suster** (sister) to talk about your immediate family.
- **Extended Family**: Use words like **oom** (uncle) and **neef** (male cousin) to talk about extended family members.
- **Parent-Child Relationships**: Words like **ouer** (parent), **kind** (child), and **seun** (son) help describe family relationships.
- **Marriage and Partners**: Use **man** (husband) and **vrou** (wife) to talk about spouses.
- **In-Laws**: Words like **skoonma** (mother-in-law) and **skoonseun** (son-in-law) help

describe relationships by marriage.

# Chapter 18

# Food and Dining: Everyday Vocabulary

Food is an important part of our daily lives, and learning how to talk about food and dining in Afrikaans will help you in many situations. Whether you are at home, at school, or eating out, knowing the words for different foods and meals is useful. In this chapter, we'll learn the Afrikaans words for different types of food, drinks, meals, and dining phrases. By the end, you'll be able to talk about food in Afrikaans!

## Basic Food Vocabulary

Let's start with the basic words for food. These are some common foods you'll see or eat every day. Here are the Afrikaans words for them:

- **brood** (pronounced: broht) – This means "bread."

- **vleis** (pronounced: flays) – This means "meat."

- **groente** (pronounced: khroon-tuh) – This means "vegetables."

- **vrugte** (pronounced: fruhkh-tuh) – This means "fruit."

- **rys** (pronounced: rays) – This means "rice."

- **eier** (pronounced: ay-er) – This means "egg."

These words will help you name common foods that are eaten every day. Here are some examples of how to use these words in sentences:

- **Ek eet brood vir ontbyt** (pronounced: ek eet broht fur ont-bayt) – This means "I eat bread for breakfast."

- **Groente is gesond** (pronounced: khroon-tuh is khuh-sont) – This means "Vegetables are healthy."

By using these words, you can talk about the foods you eat in Afrikaans.

## Fruits and Vegetables

Fruits and vegetables are an important part of a healthy diet. Let's learn the Afrikaans words for some common fruits and vegetables:

### Fruits:

- **appel** (pronounced: ah-pel) – This means "apple."

- **piesang** (pronounced: pee-sahng) – This means "banana."

- **lemoen** (pronounced: leh-moon) – This means "orange."

- **druiwe** (pronounced: dry-vuh) – This means "grapes."

- **aarbei** (pronounced: ahr-bay) – This means "strawberry."

### Vegetables:

- **wortel** (pronounced: vor-tel) – This means "carrot."

- **tamatie** (pronounced: tuh-mah-tee) – This means "tomato."

- **aartappel** (pronounced: ahrt-ah-pel) – This means "potato."

- **uie** (pronounced: ay-uh) – This means "onions."

- **spinasie** (pronounced: spi-nah-see) – This means "spinach."

Here are some sentences using these words:

- **Ek eet 'n appel vir middagete** (pronounced: ek eet uh ah-pel fur mid-ahkh-ay-tuh) – This means "I eat an apple for lunch."

- **Wortels is baie lekker** (pronounced: vor-tels is bah-ye lek-er) – This means "Carrots are very tasty."

These words will help you talk about healthy foods like fruits and vegetables in Afrikaans.

## Meals of the Day

In Afrikaans, just like in English, there are specific words for the different meals we eat throughout the day. Let's learn these words:

- **ontbyt** (pronounced: ont-bayt) – This means "breakfast."

- **middagete** (pronounced: mid-ahkh-ay-tuh) – This means "lunch."

- **aandete** (pronounced: ahnd-ay-tuh) – This means "dinner."

Here are some example sentences:

- **Ek eet ontbyt elke oggend** (pronounced: ek eet ont-bayt el-kuh oh-khond) – This means "I eat breakfast every morning."

- **Middagete is my gunsteling maaltyd** (pronounced: mid-ahkh-ay-tuh is may khun-ste-ling mahl-tayt) – This means "Lunch is my favorite meal."

These words will help you talk about the different meals you eat throughout the day.

## Drinks

When it comes to drinks, there are some common Afrikaans words that will be useful. Let's learn them:

- **water** (pronounced: vah-ter) – This means "water."

- **melk** (pronounced: melk) – This means "milk."

- **tee** (pronounced: tee) – This means "tea."

- **koffie** (pronounced: kof-fee) – This means "coffee."

- **vrugtesap** (pronounced: fruhkh-tuh-sahp) – This means "fruit juice."

Here are some example sentences using these words:

- **Ek drink water as ek dors is** (pronounced: ek drink vah-ter ahs ek dorhs is) – This means "I drink water when I am thirsty."

- **Melk is gesond** (pronounced: melk is khuh-sont) – This means "Milk is healthy."

These words will help you talk about drinks and what you like to drink in Afrikaans.

## Eating Out and Ordering Food

If you are eating out or ordering food in Afrikaans, here are some useful phrases you'll need to know:

- **Ek wil graag bestel** (pronounced: ek vul khrahkh be-stel) – This means "I would like to order."

- **Wat is op die spyskaart?** (pronounced: vaht is op dee spays-kahrt) – This means "What is on the menu?"

- **Ek wil graag 'n pizza hê** (pronounced: ek vul khrahkh uh pit-sah hay) – This means "I would like a pizza."

- **Wat kos dit?** (pronounced: vaht kos dit) – This means "How much does it cost?"

- **Dankie vir die ete** (pronounced: dahn-kee fur dee eh-tuh) – This means "Thank you for the meal."

These phrases will help you when you're at a restaurant or ordering food in Afrikaans.

## Describing Food

When talking about food, it's important to be able to describe how it tastes. Here are some Afrikaans words to describe food:

- **lekker** (pronounced: lek-er) – This means "tasty" or "delicious."

- **suur** (pronounced: see-ur) – This means "sour."

- **soet** (pronounced: soot) – This means "sweet."

- **bitter** (pronounced: bit-er) – This means "bitter."

- **pikant** (pronounced: pee-kahnt) – This means "spicy."

Here are some sentences using these words:

- **Die kos is baie lekker** (pronounced: dee kos is bah-ye lek-er) – This means "The food is very tasty."

- **Die suurlemoen is suur** (pronounced: dee see-ur-le-moon is see-ur) – This means "The lemon is sour."

These words will help you talk about what food tastes like in Afrikaans.

## Key Points to Remember

- **Basic Food Words**: Learn words like **brood** (bread) and **vleis** (meat) to talk about common foods.

- **Fruits and Vegetables**: Use words like **appel** (apple) and **wortel** (carrot) to talk about healthy fruits and vegetables.

- **Meals of the Day**: Learn words like **ontbyt** (breakfast), **middagete** (lunch), and **aandete** (dinner) to describe meals.

- **Drinks**: Use words like **water** (water) and **koffie** (coffee) to talk about what you like to drink.

- **Describing Food**: Use words like **lekker** (tasty) and **suur** (sour) to describe how food tastes.

# Chapter 19

# Colors, Shapes, and Sizes

In this chapter, we will learn how to describe things using colors, shapes, and sizes in Afrikaans. These words are important when you want to explain what something looks like or when you want to ask for something specific. By the end of this chapter, you'll know how to talk about colors, shapes, and sizes in Afrikaans with examples to help you understand better.

## Colors in Afrikaans

Colors are one of the easiest ways to describe something. Here are the common colors in Afrikaans and how to pronounce them:

- **rooi** (pronounced: roy) – This means "red."

- **blou** (pronounced: blow) – This means "blue."

- **groen** (pronounced: khroon) – This means "green."

- **geel** (pronounced: kheel) – This means "yellow."

- **swart** (pronounced: swart) – This means "black."

- **wit** (pronounced: vit) – This means "white."

- **oranje** (pronounced: oh-rah-nye) – This means "orange."

- **pienk** (pronounced: pink) – This means "pink."

- **pers** (pronounced: pers) – This means "purple."

- **grys** (pronounced: grays) – This means "gray."

Here are some sentences using these colors:

- **Die appel is rooi** (pronounced: dee ah-pel is roy) – This means "The apple is red."

- **Die blom is geel** (pronounced: dee blom is kheel) – This means "The flower is yellow."

- **Ek dra 'n blou trui** (pronounced: ek drah uh blow tray) – This means "I am wearing a blue sweater."

Knowing these colors will help you describe things you see around you.

## Talking About Shapes

Now, let's talk about shapes. Shapes help us describe the form or outline of objects. Here are some basic shapes in Afrikaans:

- **sirkel** (pronounced: sir-kel) – This means "circle."

- **vierkant** (pronounced: feer-kahnt) – This means "square."

- **driehoek** (pronounced: dree-hook) – This means "triangle."

- **reghoek** (pronounced: rehkh-hook) – This means "rectangle."

- **ovaal** (pronounced: oh-vahl) – This means "oval."

- **ster** (pronounced: stair) – This means "star."

Here are some examples of sentences using shapes:

- **Die tafel is vierkantig** (pronounced: dee tah-fel is feer-kahn-tikh) – This means "The table is square."

- **Die maan is 'n sirkel** (pronounced: dee mahn is uh sir-kel) – This means "The moon is a circle."

- **Die venster is reghoekig** (pronounced: dee fehn-ster is rehkh-hook-ikh) – This means "The window is rectangular."

These words will help you describe the shape of objects you see every day.

## Sizes in Afrikaans

Now let's talk about sizes. Whether something is big or small, sizes help us explain how large or small an object is. Here are some common words used to talk about size in Afrikaans:

- **groot** (pronounced: khroot) – This means "big" or "large."
- **klein** (pronounced: klayn) – This means "small."
- **lang** (pronounced: lahng) – This means "long."
- **kort** (pronounced: kort) – This means "short."
- **breed** (pronounced: brayt) – This means "wide."
- **nou** (pronounced: noh) – This means "narrow."

Here are some examples of sentences using sizes:

- **Die boom is groot** (pronounced: dee boom is khroot) – This means "The tree is big."
- **Die boek is klein** (pronounced: dee book is klayn) – This means "The book is small."
- **Die pad is breed** (pronounced: dee paht is brayt) – This means "The road is wide."

These size words will help you describe how large or small things are in Afrikaans.

## Combining Colors, Shapes, and Sizes

Now that you know the words for colors, shapes, and sizes, let's combine them to describe objects in more detail. For example, if you want to describe a big, blue circle, you can say:

- **Die sirkel is groot en blou** (pronounced: dee sir-kel is khroot en blow) – This means "The circle is big and blue."

Here are more examples:

- **Die reghoek is klein en groen** (pronounced: dee rehkh-hook is klayn en khroon) – This means "The rectangle is small and green."
- **Die vierkant is groot en geel** (pronounced: dee feer-kahnt is khroot en kheel) – This means "The square is big and yellow."

By combining colors, shapes, and sizes, you can describe objects in more detail and be more specific about what you see.

## Asking About Colors, Shapes, and Sizes

When talking to others, you might want to ask questions about colors, shapes, or sizes. Here are some useful questions you can ask in Afrikaans:

- **Watter kleur is dit?** (pronounced: vah-ter kleer is dit) – This means "What color is this?"

- **Watter vorm het dit?** (pronounced: vah-ter form het dit) – This means "What shape is it?"

- **Hoe groot is dit?** (pronounced: hoo khroot is dit) – This means "How big is it?"

Here are some possible answers to these questions:

- **Dit is rooi** (pronounced: dit is roy) – This means "It is red."

- **Dit is 'n sirkel** (pronounced: dit is uh sir-kel) – This means "It is a circle."

- **Dit is groot** (pronounced: dit is khroot) – This means "It is big."

These questions and answers will help you have conversations about colors, shapes, and sizes in Afrikaans.

## Key Points to Remember

- **Colors in Afrikaans**: Learn basic colors like **rooi** (red), **blou** (blue), and **geel** (yellow).

- **Shapes in Afrikaans**: Know common shapes like **sirkel** (circle), **vierkant** (square), and **driehoek** (triangle).

- **Sizes in Afrikaans**: Use words like **groot** (big) and **klein** (small) to talk about size.

- **Combining Descriptions**: Combine colors, shapes, and sizes to give more detail, like **Die sirkel is groot en blou** ("The circle is big and blue").

- **Asking Questions**: Ask questions like **Watter kleur is dit?** (What color is this?) and **Hoe groot is dit?** (How big is it?).

# Chapter 20

# Talking About Weather and Seasons

Weather and seasons are topics that we talk about almost every day. In Afrikaans, there are simple words and phrases that can help you describe the weather and talk about different seasons. In this chapter, we will learn the vocabulary for weather conditions, seasons, and how to ask and answer questions about the weather. By the end of this chapter, you will be able to talk about the weather and seasons in Afrikaans!

## Weather Vocabulary in Afrikaans

Let's begin by learning some common words to describe the weather. These words will help you explain what the weather is like on any given day:

- **weer** (pronounced: veer) – This means "weather."

- **sonnig** (pronounced: soh-nikh) – This means "sunny."

- **reënerig** (pronounced: ray-nuh-rikh) – This means "rainy."

- **bewolk** (pronounced: beh-volk) – This means "cloudy."

- **winderig** (pronounced: vin-duh-rikh) – This means "windy."

- **koud** (pronounced: kowt) – This means "cold."

- **warm** (pronounced: vah-rm) – This means "warm."

Here are some sentences you can use to describe the weather:

- **Dit is sonnig vandag** (pronounced: dit is soh-nikh fan-dahkh) – This means "It is sunny today."

- **Dit is bewolk buite** (pronounced: dit is beh-volk bay-tuh) – This means "It is cloudy outside."

- **Die weer is baie koud** (pronounced: dee veer is bah-ye kowt) – This means "The weather is very cold."

These basic words will help you talk about different weather conditions in Afrikaans.

## Describing Temperature

When talking about the weather, it's important to describe how hot or cold it is. Here are some words you can use to talk about temperature:

- **warm** (pronounced: vah-rm) – This means "warm."

- **koud** (pronounced: kowt) – This means "cold."

- **lauw** (pronounced: lahw) – This means "lukewarm" or "mild."

- **ysig** (pronounced: ay-sikh) – This means "icy" or "freezing."

Here are some example sentences:

- **Die weer is baie warm** (pronounced: dee veer is bah-ye vah-rm) – This means "The weather is very warm."

- **Dit is koud in die oggend** (pronounced: dit is kowt in dee oh-khond) – This means "It is cold in the morning."

- **Die water is ysig** (pronounced: dee vah-ter is ay-sikh) – This means "The water is freezing."

By using these words, you can describe the temperature of the weather or something else, like water.

## Talking About Seasons

Just like in English, there are four seasons in Afrikaans. Here are the Afrikaans words for the seasons:

- **lente** (pronounced: len-tuh) – This means "spring."

- **sommer** (pronounced: soh-mer) – This means "summer."

- **herfs** (pronounced: hairfs) – This means "autumn" or "fall."

- **winter** (pronounced: vin-ter) – This means "winter."

Here are some examples of how to talk about the seasons:

- **Dit is nou lente** (pronounced: dit is noh len-tuh) – This means "It is spring now."

- **Sommer is baie warm** (pronounced: soh-mer is bah-ye vah-rm) – This means "Summer is very hot."

- **Herfs is my gunsteling seisoen** (pronounced: hairfs is may khun-ste-ling say-soon) – This means "Autumn is my favorite season."

- **Winter is baie koud** (pronounced: vin-ter is bah-ye kowt) – This means "Winter is very cold."

Knowing the seasons will help you talk about what time of the year it is and describe what the weather is usually like during each season.

## Asking About the Weather

If you want to ask someone what the weather is like, here are some useful questions in Afrikaans:

- **Hoe is die weer vandag?** (pronounced: hoo is dee veer fan-dahkh) – This means "How is the weather today?"

- **Wat is die temperatuur?** (pronounced: vaht is dee tem-peh-rah-teer) – This means "What is the temperature?"

Here are some possible answers to these questions:

- **Dit is sonnig** (pronounced: dit is soh-nikh) – This means "It is sunny."

- **Dit is koud en reënerig** (pronounced: dit is kowt en ray-nuh-rikh) – This means "It is cold and rainy."

- **Die temperatuur is twintig grade** (pronounced: dee tem-peh-rah-teer is twin-tikh grah-duh) – This means "The temperature is twenty degrees."

These questions and answers will help you talk about the weather with others.

## Describing Different Types of Weather

There are many different types of weather. Here are some additional words you can use to describe the weather in Afrikaans:

- **reën** (pronounced: rayn) – This means "rain."
- **wind** (pronounced: vint) – This means "wind."
- **donderweer** (pronounced: don-der-veer) – This means "thunderstorm."
- **hael** (pronounced: hah-el) – This means "hail."
- **bewolk** (pronounced: beh-volk) – This means "cloudy."
- **son** (pronounced: son) – This means "sun."

Here are some sentences using these words:

- **Dit reën baie** (pronounced: dit rayn bah-ye) – This means "It is raining a lot."
- **Die wind waai sterk** (pronounced: dee vint vah-ee stairk) – This means "The wind is blowing strong."
- **Daar is 'n donderstorm** (pronounced: dahr is uh don-der-storm) – This means "There is a thunderstorm."
- **Die son skyn helder** (pronounced: dee son skayn hel-der) – This means "The sun is shining brightly."

These extra words will help you be more specific when describing the weather in Afrikaans.

## Talking About the Weather in Different Seasons

Different seasons have different weather patterns. Here are some sentences that describe the weather in each season:

- **Lente is lekker koel en sonnig** (pronounced: len-tuh is lek-er kool en soh-nikh) – This means "Spring is nice, cool, and sunny."
- **Sommer is baie warm en droog** (pronounced: soh-mer is bah-ye vah-rm en droo-akh) – This means "Summer is very hot and dry."
- **Herfs bring baie reën en wind** (pronounced: hairfs bring bah-ye rayn en vint) – This

means "Autumn brings a lot of rain and wind."

- **Winter is baie koud en nat** (pronounced: vin-ter is bah-ye kowt en nat) – This means "Winter is very cold and wet."

These sentences will help you talk about the typical weather during different seasons in Afrikaans.

## Key Points to Remember

- **Basic Weather Words**: Learn words like **sonnig** (sunny), **reënerig** (rainy), and **bewolk** (cloudy) to describe the weather.

- **Seasons in Afrikaans**: Know the four seasons: **lente** (spring), **sommer** (summer), **herfs** (autumn), and **winter** (winter).

- **Describing Temperature**: Use words like **warm** (warm), **koud** (cold), and **ysig** (freezing) to talk about how hot or cold it is.

- **Asking About the Weather**: Ask questions like **Hoe is die weer vandag?** (How is the weather today?) and **Wat is die temperatuur?** (What is the temperature?).

- **Talking About Different Weather Conditions**: Use words like **wind** (wind), **reën** (rain), and **donderweer** (thunderstorm) to describe different types of weather.

# Chapter 21

# Common Expressions and Phrases

When learning a new language, it's helpful to know common expressions and phrases. These are simple and useful phrases that you can use every day in conversations. In this chapter, we'll explore different ways to greet people, show politeness, express emotions, ask questions, and more in Afrikaans. By the end of this chapter, you'll be able to use these phrases in real-life situations!

## Basic Greetings

Greetings are the first things you say when you meet someone. Let's look at some basic greetings in Afrikaans:

- **Hallo** (pronounced: hah-loh) – This means "Hello."

- **Goeie môre** (pronounced: khoo-yuh mor-ruh) – This means "Good morning."

- **Goeie middag** (pronounced: khoo-yuh mid-ahkh) – This means "Good afternoon."

- **Goeie naand** (pronounced: khoo-yuh nahnt) – This means "Good evening."

- **Totsiens** (pronounced: tot-seens) – This means "Goodbye."

Here are some examples of how you can use these greetings in a conversation:

- **Hallo, hoe gaan dit?** (pronounced: hah-loh, hoo khahn dit) – This means "Hello, how are you?"

- **Goeie môre, ek hoop jy het 'n lekker dag** (pronounced: khoo-yuh mor-ruh, ek woop yay het uh lek-er dahkh) – This means "Good morning, I hope you have a nice day."

- **Totsiens, sien jou later** (pronounced: tot-seens, seen yow lah-ter) – This means "Goodbye, see you later."

Using these greetings will help you start and end conversations politely in Afrikaans.

## Polite Phrases

Politeness is important in any language. Here are some common polite expressions in Afrikaans that you can use to show respect:

- **Dankie** (pronounced: dahn-kee) – This means "Thank you."

- **Asseblief** (pronounced: ah-suh-bleef) – This means "Please."

- **Verskoon my** (pronounced: fer-skohn may) – This means "Excuse me."

- **Ek is jammer** (pronounced: ek is yah-mer) – This means "I am sorry."

Here are some examples of how to use these polite phrases:

- **Dankie vir die lekker kos** (pronounced: dahn-kee fur dee lek-er kos) – This means "Thank you for the delicious food."

- **Asseblief, kan ek dit kry?** (pronounced: ah-suh-bleef, khan ek dit kray) – This means "Please, can I have that?"

- **Verskoon my, kan ek verby kom?** (pronounced: fer-skohn may, khan ek fer-bay kom) – This means "Excuse me, can I pass by?"

Using polite phrases will make your conversations in Afrikaans more respectful and kind.

## Asking How Someone Is

Another important thing to learn is how to ask someone how they are doing. Here are some ways to ask and answer questions about how someone is feeling:

- **Hoe gaan dit?** (pronounced: hoo khahn dit) – This means "How are you?"

- **Dit gaan goed** (pronounced: dit khahn khoot) – This means "I'm doing well."

- **Ek is moeg** (pronounced: ek is moog) – This means "I am tired."

- **Ek is gelukkig** (pronounced: ek is ghe-lukh-ig) – This means "I am happy."

- **Ek voel nie goed nie** (pronounced: ek feel nee khoot nee) – This means "I don't feel well."

Here are some examples of using these phrases in a conversation:

- **Hoe gaan dit met jou?** (pronounced: hoo khahn dit met yow) – This means "How are you doing?"

- **Dit gaan baie goed, dankie** (pronounced: dit khahn bah-ye khoot, dahn-kee) – This means "I'm doing very well, thank you."

These phrases will help you start conversations by asking someone how they are and responding when they ask you.

## Introducing Yourself

When meeting someone for the first time, you'll want to introduce yourself. Here are some phrases to help you do that in Afrikaans:

- **Ek is [jou naam]** (pronounced: ek is [yow nahm]) – This means "I am [your name]."

- **Wat is jou naam?** (pronounced: vaht is yow nahm) – This means "What is your name?"

- **Aangename kennis** (pronounced: ahng-ah-nah-muh keh-nis) – This means "Nice to meet you."

Here's an example of how you can use these phrases:

- **Ek is Sarah, wat is jou naam?** (pronounced: ek is sah-rah, vaht is yow nahm) – This means "I am Sarah, what is your name?"

- **Aangename kennis, Sarah** (pronounced: ahng-ah-nah-muh keh-nis, sah-rah) – This means "Nice to meet you, Sarah."

These phrases will help you introduce yourself and get to know someone new.

## Expressing Feelings

It's also important to know how to express your feelings in Afrikaans. Here are some common phrases to help you talk about how you feel:

- **Ek is bly** (pronounced: ek is blay) – This means "I am happy."

- **Ek is hartseer** (pronounced: ek is hart-seer) – This means "I am sad."

- **Ek is kwaad** (pronounced: ek is khwahd) – This means "I am angry."

# COMMON EXPRESSIONS AND PHRASES

- **Ek is opgewonde** (pronounced: ek is op-khe-von-duh) – This means "I am excited."

- **Ek is bang** (pronounced: ek is bahng) – This means "I am scared."

Here are some examples of using these phrases:

- **Ek is bly om jou te sien** (pronounced: ek is blay om yow tuh seen) – This means "I am happy to see you."

- **Ek is hartseer oor die nuus** (pronounced: ek is hart-seer oor dee nee-uhs) – This means "I am sad about the news."

These phrases will help you express your feelings in Afrikaans and understand others when they express theirs.

## Asking for Help

Knowing how to ask for help is very important when learning a new language. Here are some phrases you can use when you need help in Afrikaans:

- **Kan jy my help?** (pronounced: khan yay may help) – This means "Can you help me?"

- **Ek het hulp nodig** (pronounced: ek het hulp noh-dikh) – This means "I need help."

- **Waar is die [iets]?** (pronounced: vahr is dee [iets]) – This means "Where is the [something]?"

Here are some examples of using these phrases:

- **Kan jy my asseblief help met my werk?** (pronounced: khan yay may ah-suh-bleef help met may verk) – This means "Can you please help me with my work?"

- **Waar is die badkamer?** (pronounced: vahr is dee baht-kah-mer) – This means "Where is the bathroom?"

Using these phrases will help you when you need assistance or directions in Afrikaans.

## Key Points to Remember

- **Greetings in Afrikaans**: Use basic greetings like **Hallo** (Hello) and **Totsiens** (Goodbye) to start and end conversations.

- **Being Polite**: Use phrases like **Dankie** (Thank you) and **Asseblief** (Please) to show politeness.

- **Asking How Someone Is**: Ask **Hoe gaan dit?** (How are you?) to check on someone's well-being, and respond with **Dit gaan goed** (I'm doing well).

- **Introducing Yourself**: Say **Ek is [jou naam]** (I am [your name]) and ask **Wat is jou naam?** (What is your name?).

- **Asking for Help**: Use phrases like **Kan jy my help?** (Can you help me?) to ask for assistance when needed.

# Chapter 22

# Modal Verbs: Can, Must, Will

Modal verbs are very important in any language because they help us talk about abilities, obligations, and future actions. In Afrikaans, modal verbs like "can," "must," and "will" are used to express what someone is able to do, what someone has to do, and what someone plans to do. In this chapter, we will learn how to use these three important modal verbs in Afrikaans: **kan** (can), **moet** (must), and **sal** (will).

## Using "Kan" (Can)

The word **kan** (pronounced: khan) in Afrikaans is used to talk about ability—what someone is able to do. It's the equivalent of the English word "can." Let's look at how to use **kan** in sentences:

- **Ek kan** (pronounced: ek khan) – This means "I can."

- **Jy kan** (pronounced: yay khan) – This means "You can."

- **Hy kan** (pronounced: hay khan) – This means "He can."

Here are some example sentences using **kan**:

- **Ek kan Afrikaans praat** (pronounced: ek khan ah-free-kahns praht) – This means "I can speak Afrikaans."

- **Sy kan vinnig hardloop** (pronounced: say khan fin-nikh har-dloop) – This means "She can run fast."

- **Ons kan later gaan** (pronounced: ohns khan lah-ter khaan) – This means "We can go later."

As you can see, **kan** is used to show what you or someone else is able to do. You simply put **kan** in front of the verb you want to describe.

## Using "Moet" (Must)

The word **moet** (pronounced: moot) in Afrikaans is used to talk about something that has to be done, just like the English word "must." It shows obligation or necessity. Here's how to use **moet**:

- **Ek moet** (pronounced: ek moot) – This means "I must."

- **Jy moet** (pronounced: yay moot) – This means "You must."

- **Hulle moet** (pronounced: huh-luh moot) – This means "They must."

Here are some examples using **moet** in sentences:

- **Ek moet my huiswerk doen** (pronounced: ek moot may hays-verk doon) – This means "I must do my homework."

- **Jy moet betyds wees** (pronounced: yay moot beh-tays vees) – This means "You must be on time."

- **Ons moet vandag die taak voltooi** (pronounced: ohns moot fan-dahkh dee tahk fol-toy) – This means "We must finish the task today."

As you can see, **moet** is used when something is necessary or has to be done. It always comes before the main verb in the sentence.

## Using "Sal" (Will)

The word **sal** (pronounced: sul) is used to talk about future actions or things that will happen. It's the Afrikaans word for "will." Here's how to use **sal**:

- **Ek sal** (pronounced: ek sul) – This means "I will."

- **Jy sal** (pronounced: yay sul) – This means "You will."

- **Hulle sal** (pronounced: huh-luh sul) – This means "They will."

Here are some example sentences using **sal**:

- **Ek sal more kom** (pronounced: ek sul moh-ruh kom) – This means "I will come tomorrow."

- **Sy sal haar boek bring** (pronounced: say sul hahr book bring) – This means "She will bring her book."

- **Ons sal saam gaan** (pronounced: ohns sul sahm khaan) – This means "We will go together."

When using **sal**, you are talking about things that will happen in the future. Like other modal verbs, **sal** is placed before the main verb in the sentence.

## Forming Questions with Modal Verbs

You can also use modal verbs to ask questions. To do this, you place the modal verb at the beginning of the sentence. Let's look at how to ask questions using **kan**, **moet**, and **sal**:

- **Kan ek jou help?** (pronounced: khan ek yow help) – This means "Can I help you?"

- **Moet ons nou gaan?** (pronounced: moot ohns noh khaan) – This means "Must we go now?"

- **Sal jy more kom?** (pronounced: sul yay moh-ruh kom) – This means "Will you come tomorrow?"

By starting the sentence with the modal verb, you can easily turn it into a question. This is a simple and effective way to ask about abilities, obligations, and future plans in Afrikaans.

## Negative Sentences with Modal Verbs

To make negative sentences with modal verbs in Afrikaans, you simply add the word **nie** (pronounced: nee) after the verb and at the end of the sentence. Let's look at some examples:

- **Ek kan nie sing nie** (pronounced: ek khan nee sing nee) – This means "I cannot sing."

- **Hy moet nie laat wees nie** (pronounced: hay moot nee laht vees nee) – This means "He must not be late."

- **Ons sal nie gaan nie** (pronounced: ohns sul nee khaan nee) – This means "We will not go."

As you can see, you add **nie** after the verb and again at the end of the sentence to create a negative sentence with modal verbs in Afrikaans.

## Key Points to Remember

- **Kan means "can"**: Use **kan** to talk about abilities, like **Ek kan Afrikaans praat** ("I can speak Afrikaans").

- **Moet means "must"**: Use **moet** to talk about obligations, like **Ek moet my werk doen** ("I must do my work").

- **Sal means "will"**: Use **sal** to talk about future actions, like **Ek sal kom** ("I will come").

- **Questions with modal verbs**: To ask a question, start with the modal verb, like **Kan ek jou help?** ("Can I help you?").

- **Negative sentences**: To form a negative sentence, use **nie** after the verb and at the end, like **Ek kan nie sing nie** ("I cannot sing").

# Chapter 23

# Prepositions: In, On, Under, Around

Prepositions are small words that help us understand the relationship between objects, places, and people. In Afrikaans, just like in English, prepositions tell us where things are or how they are positioned in relation to each other. Some common prepositions are "in," "on," "under," and "around." In this chapter, we will learn how to use these prepositions in Afrikaans, with examples to help you understand their meanings.

## Using "In" (In)

The Afrikaans word for "in" is **in** (pronounced: in). It is used just like the English word "in," and it shows that something is inside something else. Let's look at some examples of how to use **in** in Afrikaans:

- **Die boek is in die tas** (pronounced: dee book is in dee tahs) – This means "The book is in the bag."

- **Ek is in die huis** (pronounced: ek is in dee hays) – This means "I am in the house."

- **Die kat is in die boks** (pronounced: dee kaht is in dee boks) – This means "The cat is in the box."

As you can see, the preposition **in** is used to show that something is located inside another object or place. You simply place it before the location or object.

## Using "Op" (On)

The Afrikaans word for "on" is **op** (pronounced: op). It is used when something is located on the surface of something else. Let's look at how to use **op** in Afrikaans:

- **Die boek is op die tafel** (pronounced: dee book is op dee tah-fel) – This means "The book is on the table."

- **Die bord is op die stoel** (pronounced: dee bort is op dee stuhl) – This means "The plate is on the chair."

- **Sy sit op die bed** (pronounced: say sit op dee bed) – This means "She is sitting on the bed."

Using **op** is simple. It always goes before the noun it refers to and tells us that something is located on a surface.

## Using "Onder" (Under)

The Afrikaans word for "under" is **onder** (pronounced: on-der). It is used to describe when something is located beneath or below another object. Let's look at some examples:

- **Die hond is onder die tafel** (pronounced: dee hond is on-der dee tah-fel) – This means "The dog is under the table."

- **Die bal is onder die stoel** (pronounced: dee bahl is on-der dee stuhl) – This means "The ball is under the chair."

- **Ek is onder die sambreel** (pronounced: ek is on-der dee sahm-breel) – This means "I am under the umbrella."

In each of these sentences, **onder** is used to show that something is located beneath another object. Just like with other prepositions, you place it before the object.

## Using "Om" (Around)

The Afrikaans word for "around" is **om** (pronounced: om). It shows that something is positioned in a circular way or all around something else. Here are some examples of how to use **om** in Afrikaans:

- **Die kinders hardloop om die boom** (pronounced: dee kin-ders har-dloop om dee bohm) – This means "The children are running around the tree."

- **Daar is 'n heining om die tuin** (pronounced: dahr is uh hay-ning om dee tayn) – This means "There is a fence around the garden."

- **Sy draai om die huis** (pronounced: say drah-ee om dee hays) – This means "She is walking around the house."

**Om** is used to describe something that is going around or surrounding another object. It's very useful for talking about movement or things that go in circles.

## Combining Prepositions in Sentences

Now that we know how to use **in**, **op**, **onder**, and **om**, let's combine them in sentences to give more detailed descriptions of where things are. For example:

- **Die kat slaap op die bed onder die komberse** (pronounced: dee kaht slahp op dee bed on-der dee kom-bair-suh) – This means "The cat is sleeping on the bed under the blankets."

- **Ek sit in die kamer om die tafel** (pronounced: ek sit in dee kah-mer om dee tah-fel) – This means "I am sitting in the room around the table."

By combining prepositions, you can give more specific information about the position of things in Afrikaans.

## Asking Questions with Prepositions

You can also use prepositions to ask questions about where something is located. Here are some examples of questions using the prepositions **in**, **op**, **onder**, and **om**:

- **Waar is die boek? Is dit op die tafel?** (pronounced: vahr is dee book? Is dit op dee tah-fel) – This means "Where is the book? Is it on the table?"

- **Is die bal onder die stoel?** (pronounced: is dee bahl on-der dee stuhl) – This means "Is the ball under the chair?"

- **Loop jy om die park?** (pronounced: lohp yay om dee park) – This means "Are you walking around the park?"

These questions show how you can use prepositions to ask about the location of something in Afrikaans.

## Negative Sentences with Prepositions

To make a negative sentence with prepositions in Afrikaans, you add the word **nie** after the verb and at the end of the sentence. Let's look at some examples:

- **Die boek is nie op die tafel nie** (pronounced: dee book is nee op dee tah-fel nee) – This means "The book is not on the table."

- **Die bal is nie onder die stoel nie** (pronounced: dee bahl is nee on-der dee stuhl nee) – This means "The ball is not under the chair."

In these sentences, the word **nie** is used twice to turn the statement into a negative sentence. It tells us that something is not in the place we expect it to be.

## Key Points to Remember

- **In means "in"**: Use **in** to show that something is inside something else, like **Die boek is in die tas** ("The book is in the bag").

- **Op means "on"**: Use **op** to show that something is on top of something, like **Die boek is op die tafel** ("The book is on the table").

- **Onder means "under"**: Use **onder** to show that something is beneath something, like **Die hond is onder die tafel** ("The dog is under the table").

- **Om means "around"**: Use **om** to describe something going around or surrounding something else, like **Die kinders hardloop om die boom** ("The children are running around the tree").

- **Negative sentences**: Add **nie** after the verb and at the end to make a sentence negative, like **Die boek is nie op die tafel nie** ("The book is not on the table").

# Chapter 24

# Making Comparisons: Bigger, Smaller, Faster

When we want to compare two or more things, we use special words called comparatives. In Afrikaans, just like in English, we can compare the size, speed, or qualities of objects and people. Comparatives help us describe how one thing is different from another, such as saying something is bigger, smaller, or faster. In this chapter, we will learn how to make comparisons in Afrikaans and use them in sentences. By the end, you will be able to compare things confidently in Afrikaans!

## Understanding Comparatives

In Afrikaans, comparatives are used to compare two things. When you want to say that something is bigger, smaller, or faster than something else, you add a special ending to the adjective or use a specific word. Just like in English, Afrikaans comparatives often end with **-er**, but there are some differences.

Let's begin by learning how to form basic comparatives in Afrikaans.

## Comparing Sizes: Bigger and Smaller

To compare the size of two things, you can use the words **groter** (pronounced: khroo-ter) for "bigger" and **kleiner** (pronounced: klay-ner) for "smaller." Let's look at some examples of how to use these comparatives:

- **groter** – This means "bigger."
- **kleiner** – This means "smaller."

Here are some examples of sentences comparing sizes:

- **Die hond is groter as die kat** (pronounced: dee hond is khroo-ter ahs dee kaht) – This means "The dog is bigger than the cat."

- **Die potlood is kleiner as die pen** (pronounced: dee pot-lood is klay-ner ahs dee pen) – This means "The pencil is smaller than the pen."

- **My huis is groter as jou huis** (pronounced: may hays is khroo-ter ahs yow hays) – This means "My house is bigger than your house."

As you can see, when you want to compare two things, you add **-er** to the adjective. You also use the word **as** (pronounced: ahs), which means "than," to show the comparison.

## Comparing Speed: Faster and Slower

To compare how fast something moves, you can use the words **vinniger** (pronounced: fin-nikh-er) for "faster" and **stadiger** (pronounced: stah-dikh-er) for "slower." Let's look at how to use these comparatives:

- **vinniger** – This means "faster."

- **stadiger** – This means "slower."

Here are some examples of sentences comparing speed:

- **Ek hardloop vinniger as jy** (pronounced: ek har-dloop fin-nikh-er ahs yay) – This means "I run faster than you."

- **Die skilpad is stadiger as die haas** (pronounced: dee skil-pahd is stah-dikh-er ahs dee hahs) – This means "The turtle is slower than the hare."

- **Sy fiets is vinniger as my fiets** (pronounced: say fits is fin-nikh-er ahs may fits) – This means "Her bicycle is faster than my bicycle."

Just like with size comparisons, you use the word **as** to connect the two things you are comparing. The word **vinniger** means "faster," and **stadiger** means "slower."

## Comparing Height: Taller and Shorter

Another common comparison is height. To compare how tall or short someone is, you can use the words **langer** (pronounced: lahng-er) for "taller" and **korter** (pronounced: kor-ter) for "shorter." Here's how to use them:

- **langer** – This means "taller."

- **korter** – This means "shorter."

Here are some examples of sentences comparing height:

- **Ek is langer as my broer** (pronounced: ek is lahng-er ahs may broor) – This means "I am taller than my brother."

- **Sy is korter as haar suster** (pronounced: say is kor-ter ahs hahr sus-ter) – This means "She is shorter than her sister."

In each of these examples, you are comparing the height of two people, using **langer** for "taller" and **korter** for "shorter."

## Comparing Age: Older and Younger

To compare age, you can use the words **ouer** (pronounced: oh-er) for "older" and **jonger** (pronounced: yohng-er) for "younger." Let's see how these words are used in sentences:

- **ouer** – This means "older."

- **jonger** – This means "younger."

Here are some example sentences comparing age:

- **Ek is ouer as jy** (pronounced: ek is oh-er ahs yay) – This means "I am older than you."

- **Sy is jonger as haar broer** (pronounced: say is yohng-er ahs hahr broor) – This means "She is younger than her brother."

Comparing age in Afrikaans is easy. You use **ouer** for "older" and **jonger** for "younger," just like in English.

## Irregular Comparatives

In Afrikaans, some comparatives do not follow the regular pattern of adding **-er**. These are called irregular comparatives. Let's look at some examples of irregular comparatives:

- **goed** becomes **beter** (pronounced: bay-ter) – This means "better."

- **sleg** becomes **slegter** (pronounced: slekh-ter) – This means "worse."

- **veel** becomes **meer** (pronounced: meer) – This means "more."

- **min** becomes **minder** (pronounced: min-der) – This means "less."

Here are some examples using irregular comparatives in sentences:

- **Die weer is beter vandag** (pronounced: dee veer is bay-ter fan-dahkh) – This means "The weather is better today."

- **Hierdie kos is slegter as die vorige keer** (pronounced: heer-dee kos is slekh-ter ahs dee for-uh-khe keer) – This means "This food is worse than the last time."

Irregular comparatives, like **beter** for "better" and **slegter** for "worse," do not follow the usual pattern but are important to remember when making comparisons.

## Forming Questions with Comparatives

You can also ask questions using comparatives. Here's how you can form questions to compare two things in Afrikaans:

- **Wie is groter, jy of ek?** (pronounced: vee is khroo-ter, yay off ek) – This means "Who is bigger, you or me?"

- **Is die hond vinniger as die kat?** (pronounced: is dee hond fin-nikh-er ahs dee kaht) – This means "Is the dog faster than the cat?"

These questions help you ask about size, speed, or other comparisons between two things or people.

## Key Points to Remember

- **Add -er to form comparatives:** In Afrikaans, comparatives often end in **-er**, like **groter** (bigger) and **kleiner** (smaller).

- **Use "as" for comparisons:** When comparing two things, use the word as, like **Ek is groter as jy** ("I am bigger than you").

- **Some comparatives are irregular:** Words like **beter** (better) and **slegter** (worse) do not follow the regular pattern.

- **Use comparatives to compare qualities:** You can compare size, speed, age, and more by using comparatives in your sentences.

- **Ask questions with comparatives:** You can ask questions like **Wie is groter?** ("Who is bigger?") to compare two people or things.

# Chapter 25

# Talking About Daily Activities and Routines

Being able to talk about your daily activities and routines is an important part of learning a new language. In Afrikaans, you will need to know some key vocabulary and phrases to describe what you do every day, from getting up in the morning to going to bed at night. In this chapter, we will learn how to talk about common daily activities and routines, giving you the tools to describe your day in Afrikaans.

## Morning Activities

Let's start by learning some useful phrases to talk about what you do in the morning. Here are some common activities people do when they wake up:

- **Ek staan op** (pronounced: ek stahn op) – This means "I get up."

- **Ek maak my bed op** (pronounced: ek mahk may bed op) – This means "I make my bed."

- **Ek eet ontbyt** (pronounced: ek eet ont-bayt) – This means "I eat breakfast."

- **Ek borsel my tande** (pronounced: ek bor-sel may tan-de) – This means "I brush my teeth."

- **Ek trek my klere aan** (pronounced: ek trek may klee-ruh ahn) – This means "I put on my clothes."

Here are some example sentences using these morning activity phrases:

- **Ek staan elke oggend vroeg op** (pronounced: ek stahn el-kuh oh-khond fruhkh op) – This means "I get up early every morning."

- **Ek eet ontbyt saam met my gesin** (pronounced: ek eet ont-bayt sahm met may khuh-sin) – This means "I eat breakfast with my family."

These phrases will help you describe what you do to start your day in Afrikaans.

## School and Work Activities

After getting ready in the morning, many people go to school or work. Here are some useful phrases to talk about what you do during school or work:

- **Ek gaan skool toe** (pronounced: ek khaan skohl too) – This means "I go to school."

- **Ek werk by die rekenaar** (pronounced: ek verk bay dee ray-kuh-nahr) – This means "I work on the computer."

- **Ek leer in die klas** (pronounced: ek leer in dee klahs) – This means "I learn in the classroom."

- **Ek doen my huiswerk** (pronounced: ek doon may hays-verk) – This means "I do my homework."

- **Ek praat met my vriende** (pronounced: ek praht met may free-nde) – This means "I talk to my friends."

Here are some examples of sentences using these school and work phrases:

- **Ek gaan elke dag skool toe** (pronounced: ek khaan el-kuh dahkh skohl too) – This means "I go to school every day."

- **Ek doen my huiswerk na skool** (pronounced: ek doon may hays-verk nah skohl) – This means "I do my homework after school."

These phrases will help you talk about what you do during your day at school or work.

## Afternoon and Evening Activities

In the afternoon and evening, people often relax, eat dinner, and spend time with their families. Here are some useful phrases to talk about your afternoon and evening activities:

- **Ek eet middagete** (pronounced: ek eet mid-ahkh-ay-tuh) – This means "I eat lunch."

- **Ek speel buite** (pronounced: ek speel bay-tuh) – This means "I play outside."

- **Ek kyk televisie** (pronounced: ek kayk tel-uh-vee-zee) – This means "I watch television."

- **Ek eet aandete** (pronounced: ek eet ahnd-ay-tuh) – This means "I eat dinner."

- **Ek gesels met my gesin** (pronounced: ek khuh-sels met may khuh-sin) – This means "I chat with my family."

Here are some example sentences using these phrases:

- **Na middagete speel ek buite met my vriende** (pronounced: nah mid-ahkh-ay-tuh speel ek bay-tuh met may free-nde) – This means "After lunch, I play outside with my friends."

- **Ek kyk televisie elke aand** (pronounced: ek kayk tel-uh-vee-zee el-kuh ahnd) – This means "I watch television every evening."

These phrases will help you talk about your afternoon and evening activities in Afrikaans.

## Nighttime Routine

Finally, let's learn how to talk about what you do before going to bed. Here are some useful phrases to describe your nighttime routine:

- **Ek borsel my tande** (pronounced: ek bor-sel may tan-de) – This means "I brush my teeth."

- **Ek trek my slaapklere aan** (pronounced: ek trek may slahp-klee-ruh ahn) – This means "I put on my pajamas."

- **Ek lees 'n boek** (pronounced: ek lees uh book) – This means "I read a book."

- **Ek gaan slaap** (pronounced: ek khaan slahp) – This means "I go to sleep."

Here are some example sentences using these nighttime routine phrases:

- **Ek lees 'n boek voor ek gaan slaap** (pronounced: ek lees uh book fohr ek khaan slahp) – This means "I read a book before I go to sleep."

- **Ek borsel my tande elke aand** (pronounced: ek bor-sel may tan-de el-kuh ahnd) – This means "I brush my teeth every night."

These phrases will help you talk about what you do to get ready for bed in Afrikaans.

## Talking About Your Routine

Now that we've learned some useful vocabulary, let's practice talking about your daily routine. Here's an example of how you can describe your entire day in Afrikaans:

- **Ek staan elke oggend vroeg op** (pronounced: ek stahn el-kuh oh-khond fruhkh op) – This means "I get up early every morning."

- **Ek eet ontbyt en gaan skool toe** (pronounced: ek eet ont-bayt en khaan skohl too) – This means "I eat breakfast and go to school."

- **Ek leer in die klas en doen my huiswerk** (pronounced: ek leer in dee klahs en doon may hays-verk) – This means "I learn in the classroom and do my homework."

- **Na middagete speel ek buite** (pronounced: nah mid-ahkh-ay-tuh speel ek bay-tuh) – This means "After lunch, I play outside."

- **Ek kyk televisie en gesels met my gesin** (pronounced: ek kayk tel-uh-vee-zee en khuh-sels met may khuh-sin) – This means "I watch television and chat with my family."

- **Ek borsel my tande en gaan slaap** (pronounced: ek bor-sel may tan-de en khaan slahp) – This means "I brush my teeth and go to sleep."

This example shows how you can talk about your daily routine from morning to night in Afrikaans. Feel free to change the activities to match your own routine.

## Key Points to Remember

- **Morning activities**: Use phrases like **Ek staan op** ("I get up") and **Ek eet ontbyt** ("I eat breakfast") to describe your morning routine.

- **School and work activities** : Use phrases like **Ek gaan skool toe** ("I go to school") and **Ek doen my huiswerk** ("I do my homework") to talk about your day at school or work.

- **Afternoon and evening activities**: Talk about what you do in the afternoon and evening with phrases like **Ek speel buite** ("I play outside") and **Ek kyk televisie** ("I watch TV").

- **Nighttime routine**: Use phrases like **Ek borsel my tande** ("I brush my teeth") and **Ek gaan slaap** ("I go to sleep") to describe your night routine.

- **Daily routine**: Combine these phrases to describe your entire day from morning to night.

# Chapter 26

# Adverbs: Time, Place, and Manner

Adverbs are words that help describe how, when, or where something happens. In Afrikaans, adverbs work the same way as in English. They can tell us more about an action, such as when it happened (time), where it happened (place), or how it happened (manner). In this chapter, we will explore different types of adverbs in Afrikaans and learn how to use them in sentences to make our descriptions clearer and more detailed.

## Adverbs of Time

Adverbs of time tell us when something happens. These words are used to describe the time of an action, whether it happens today, yesterday, tomorrow, or at some other point in time. Here are some common adverbs of time in Afrikaans:

- **vandag** (pronounced: fan-dahkh) – This means "today."

- **gister** (pronounced: khis-ter) – This means "yesterday."

- **more** (pronounced: moh-ruh) – This means "tomorrow."

- **nou** (pronounced: noh) – This means "now."

- **later** (pronounced: lah-ter) – This means "later."

- **binnekort** (pronounced: bin-nuh-kort) – This means "soon."

Here are some examples of how to use adverbs of time in sentences:

- **Ek gaan vandag skool toe** (pronounced: ek khaan fan-dahkh skohl too) – This means "I am going to school today."

- **Ons het gister 'n boek gelees** (pronounced: ohns het khis-ter uh book khuh-lees) – This means "We read a book yesterday."

- **Sy sal more kom** (pronounced: say sul moh-ruh kom) – This means "She will come tomorrow."

Adverbs of time are placed after the verb or at the beginning of the sentence, just like in English. They are very useful for talking about when things happen.

## Adverbs of Place

Adverbs of place describe where something happens or where someone or something is located. They tell us the location of an action. Here are some common adverbs of place in Afrikaans:

- **hier** (pronounced: heer) – This means "here."
- **daar** (pronounced: dahr) – This means "there."
- **oral** (pronounced: oh-rahl) – This means "everywhere."
- **binne** (pronounced: bin-nuh) – This means "inside."
- **buite** (pronounced: bay-tuh) – This means "outside."
- **bo** (pronounced: boh) – This means "above."
- **onder** (pronounced: on-der) – This means "below" or "under."

Here are some examples of how to use adverbs of place in sentences:

- **Die kinders speel hier** (pronounced: dee kin-ders speel heer) – This means "The children are playing here."
- **Die kat is daar** (pronounced: dee kaht is dahr) – This means "The cat is there."
- **Ek werk binne** (pronounced: ek verk bin-nuh) – This means "I am working inside."

Adverbs of place usually come after the verb or at the end of the sentence. They help us explain where something is happening.

## Adverbs of Manner

Adverbs of manner describe how something happens or how someone does something. These adverbs give more information about the way an action is performed. Here are some common adverbs of manner in Afrikaans:

- **vinnig** (pronounced: fin-nikh) – This means "quickly."
- **stadig** (pronounced: stah-dikh) – This means "slowly."
- **hard** (pronounced: hahrt) – This means "hard" or "loudly."
- **sag** (pronounced: sakh) – This means "softly."
- **goed** (pronounced: khoot) – This means "well."
- **sleg** (pronounced: slekh) – This means "badly."

Here are some examples of how to use adverbs of manner in sentences:

- **Hy loop vinnig** (pronounced: hay lohp fin-nikh) – This means "He walks quickly."
- **Ek praat sag** (pronounced: ek praht sakh) – This means "I speak softly."
- **Sy sing baie goed** (pronounced: say sing bah-ye khoot) – This means "She sings very well."

Adverbs of manner usually come after the verb, but sometimes they can also be placed at the end of the sentence. They are useful for describing how someone does something.

## Forming Sentences with Adverbs

Now that we know how to use adverbs of time, place, and manner, let's practice combining them in sentences. Here are some examples that use multiple types of adverbs:

- **Ek sal more vinnig skool toe gaan** (pronounced: ek sul moh-ruh fin-nikh skohl too khaan) – This means "I will go to school quickly tomorrow."
- **Die kinders speel buite vandag** (pronounced: dee kin-ders speel bay-tuh fan-dahkh) – This means "The children are playing outside today."
- **Hy sing baie hard hier** (pronounced: hay sing bah-ye hahrt heer) – This means "He sings very loudly here."

In these sentences, you can see how adverbs of time, place, and manner can work together to give more details about the action. The adverb of time usually comes first, followed by the adverb of manner and then the adverb of place, but this order can sometimes change.

## Asking Questions with Adverbs

Adverbs are also helpful when asking questions. Here are some examples of questions you can ask using adverbs of time, place, and manner:

- **Wanneer kom jy?** (pronounced: vah-nehr kom yay) – This means "When are you coming?"

- **Waar is die boek?** (pronounced: vahr is dee book) – This means "Where is the book?"

- **Hoe loop sy?** (pronounced: hoo lohp say) – This means "How does she walk?"

These questions use adverbs to ask about the time, place, and manner of an action. You can answer them by using the appropriate adverb in your response.

## Negative Sentences with Adverbs

In Afrikaans, you can also use adverbs in negative sentences. To make a sentence negative, you add the word **nie** after the verb and at the end of the sentence. Here are some examples:

- **Ek gaan nie vandag skool toe nie** (pronounced: ek khaan nee fan-dahkh skohl too nee) – This means "I am not going to school today."

- **Hy sing nie hard hier nie** (pronounced: hay sing nee hahrt heer nee) – This means "He does not sing loudly here."

- **Ons werk nie binne nie** (pronounced: ohns verk nee bin-nuh nee) – This means "We do not work inside."

In these sentences, the word **nie** is used twice to make the sentence negative while still using the adverb. This is how you can form negative sentences with adverbs in Afrikaans.

## Key Points to Remember

- **Adverbs of time**: Use words like **vandag** (today), **gister** (yesterday), and **more** (tomorrow) to describe when something happens.

- **Adverbs of place**: Use words like **hier** (here), **daar** (there), and **buite** (outside) to describe where something happens.

- **Adverbs of manner**: Use words like **vinnig** (quickly), **stadig** (slowly), and **hard** (loudly) to describe how something happens.

- **Questions with adverbs**: You can ask questions with adverbs, like **Wanneer kom jy?** (When are you coming?) and **Waar is die boek?** (Where is the book?).

- **Negative sentences**: To make a sentence negative with adverbs, add **nie** after the verb and at the end of the sentence, like **Ek gaan nie vandag nie** (I am not going today).

# Chapter 27

# The Present Tense: Basic Conjugation

The present tense is one of the most important tenses in any language because it helps us talk about things that are happening right now or things that happen regularly. In Afrikaans, the present tense is quite simple to form and use. In this chapter, we will learn how to conjugate verbs in the present tense, and we will go over some examples to help you understand how to use them in sentences. By the end of this chapter, you will be able to talk about actions happening in the present in Afrikaans.

## What is the Present Tense?

The present tense is used to describe actions that are happening now or actions that happen regularly. In English, we say things like "I eat," "She walks," or "They play" to talk about the present tense. In Afrikaans, the way we form the present tense is a little different from English, but it is straightforward once you know the basic rules.

## Conjugating Regular Verbs

In Afrikaans, many verbs follow a regular pattern when conjugating them in the present tense. The good news is that the verb does not change for different subjects like it does in English. For example, in English, we say "I walk" but "He walks," where the verb changes. In Afrikaans, the verb stays the same for every subject. Let's look at some examples:

- **Ek eet** (pronounced: ek eet) – This means "I eat."

- **Jy eet** (pronounced: yay eet) – This means "You eat."

- **Hy eet** (pronounced: hay eet) – This means "He eats."

- **Sy eet** (pronounced: say eet) – This means "She eats."

- **Ons eet** (pronounced: ohns eet) – This means "We eat."

- **Hulle eet** (pronounced: huh-luh eet) – This means "They eat."

As you can see, the verb **eet** (to eat) stays the same no matter who is doing the action. This makes learning Afrikaans verbs in the present tense much easier than in some other languages.

## Using Verbs in Sentences

Now that we know how to conjugate regular verbs in the present tense, let's see how they are used in sentences. Here are some examples of simple present tense sentences:

- **Ek speel sokker** (pronounced: ek speel soh-ker) – This means "I play soccer."

- **Sy lees 'n boek** (pronounced: say lees uh book) – This means "She reads a book."

- **Ons drink water** (pronounced: ohns dring vah-ter) – This means "We drink water."

In each of these examples, the verb is in the present tense, showing that the action is happening now. Notice how the verb doesn't change depending on the subject—it stays the same no matter who is doing the action.

## Conjugating Irregular Verbs

While most verbs in Afrikaans follow regular patterns, there are some irregular verbs that you need to learn. Irregular verbs don't follow the usual rules, so their conjugations might be a little different. Here are a few common irregular verbs in the present tense:

- **Ek is** (pronounced: ek is) – This means "I am."

- **Jy is** (pronounced: yay is) – This means "You are."

- **Hy is** (pronounced: hay is) – This means "He is."

- **Ons is** (pronounced: ohns is) – This means "We are."

Another common irregular verb is **hê** (to have):

- **Ek het** (pronounced: ek het) – This means "I have."

- **Jy het** (pronounced: yay het) – This means "You have."

- **Sy het** (pronounced: say het) – This means "She has."

- **Hulle het** (pronounced: huh-luh het) – This means "They have."

Even though these verbs don't follow the regular conjugation rules, they are easy to remember with a little practice.

## Negative Sentences in the Present Tense

To make a sentence negative in Afrikaans, you need to add the word **nie** (pronounced: nee) after the verb and at the end of the sentence. Here are some examples:

- **Ek lees nie 'n boek nie** (pronounced: ek lees nee uh book nee) – This means "I am not reading a book."
- **Ons eet nie nou nie** (pronounced: ohns eet nee noh nee) – This means "We are not eating now."
- **Sy speel nie sokker nie** (pronounced: say speel nee soh-ker nee) – This means "She is not playing soccer."

As you can see, the word **nie** is used twice to turn the sentence into a negative. You place the first **nie** right after the verb and the second **nie** at the end of the sentence.

## Asking Questions in the Present Tense

In Afrikaans, you can ask questions in the present tense by changing the word order or by using question words. Here are some examples of questions:

- **Lees jy 'n boek?** (pronounced: lees yay uh book) – This means "Are you reading a book?"
- **Wat doen jy?** (pronounced: vaht doon yay) – This means "What are you doing?"
- **Is hy by die huis?** (pronounced: is hay bay dee hays) – This means "Is he at home?"

Notice that for yes/no questions, you can simply change the word order, while for questions using words like **wat** (what) or **waar** (where), you put the question word at the beginning of the sentence.

## Common Present Tense Verbs

Let's review some common verbs in Afrikaans that you can use in the present tense. These verbs are regular and easy to conjugate:

- **praat** (pronounced: praht) – This means "to speak."

- **leer** (pronounced: leer) – This means "to learn."

- **werk** (pronounced: verk) – This means "to work."

- **kyk** (pronounced: kayk) – This means "to watch."

- **speel** (pronounced: speel) – This means "to play."

Here are some example sentences using these verbs in the present tense:

- **Ek praat met my vriend** (pronounced: ek praht met may freend) – This means "I am talking to my friend."

- **Sy leer elke dag** (pronounced: say leer el-kuh dahkh) – This means "She learns every day."

- **Ons werk saam** (pronounced: ohns verk sahm) – This means "We are working together."

By using these common verbs, you can start talking about many different actions in Afrikaans.

## Key Points to Remember

- **Present tense verbs stay the same for all subjects**: In Afrikaans, the verb doesn't change based on who is doing the action, making it easier to conjugate verbs.

- **Irregular verbs need to be memorized**: Some verbs, like **is** (am/are) and **het** (have), are irregular and don't follow the regular rules.

- **Negative sentences use "nie" twice**: To make a sentence negative, place **nie** after the verb and again at the end of the sentence.

- **Questions can change word order**: For yes/no questions, simply switch the word order, or use question words like **wat** (what) and **waar** (where).

- **Common present tense verbs**: Start using regular verbs like **praat** (speak), **leer** (learn), and **speel** (play) in your daily conversations.

# Chapter 28

# The Past Tense: Describing What Happened

When we talk about things that happened in the past, we use the past tense. In Afrikaans, the past tense is used to describe actions or events that have already happened. Learning the past tense will help you tell stories, talk about your day, or describe things that happened yesterday or even long ago. In this chapter, we will explore how to form the past tense in Afrikaans, and we will look at some examples to help you understand how to use it in sentences.

## Forming the Past Tense

In Afrikaans, the past tense is typically formed using the word **het** (pronounced: het), which means "have," and a verb that begins with **ge-**. Let's start with an example:

- **Ek het gespeel** (pronounced: ek het khuh-speel) – This means "I played."

In this sentence, **het** is used to indicate that the action happened in the past, and the verb **speel** (to play) gets the prefix **ge-** added to it to form the past tense. The basic structure for past tense sentences in Afrikaans is:

**[Subject] + het + [verb with ge- prefix]**

Let's look at some more examples to see how this works:

- **Ek het gelees** (pronounced: ek het khuh-lees) – This means "I read" (in the past).
- **Hy het gedrink** (pronounced: hay het khuh-drink) – This means "He drank."
- **Sy het gewerk** (pronounced: say het khuh-verk) – This means "She worked."

As you can see, the verb in each sentence has the **ge-** prefix to show that the action happened in the past. The word **het** stays the same for all subjects (I, you, he, she, we, they).

## Using Verbs in the Past Tense

Now that we understand the basic structure of the past tense in Afrikaans, let's see how we can use it in sentences to describe what happened. Here are some example sentences using the past tense:

- **Ek het my huiswerk gedoen** (pronounced: ek het may hays-verk khuh-doon) – This means "I did my homework."

- **Ons het televisie gekyk** (pronounced: ohns het tel-uh-vee-zee khuh-kayk) – This means "We watched television."

- **Hy het sokker gespeel** (pronounced: hay het soh-ker khuh-speel) – This means "He played soccer."

In each of these sentences, the verb is in the past tense, and the action has already happened. This is how you describe past events in Afrikaans using the basic **het** + **ge-** structure.

## Irregular Verbs in the Past Tense

Just like in English, Afrikaans has some irregular verbs that don't follow the regular rules for forming the past tense. These irregular verbs do not take the **ge-** prefix. Here are a few common irregular verbs in the past tense:

- **Ek was** (pronounced: ek vahs) – This means "I was."

- **Jy was** (pronounced: yay vahs) – This means "You were."

- **Hy was** (pronounced: hay vahs) – This means "He was."

Another common irregular verb is **hê** (to have):

- **Ek het gehad** (pronounced: ek het khuh-haht) – This means "I had."

- **Sy het gehad** (pronounced: say het khuh-haht) – This means "She had."

These irregular verbs do not use the **ge-** prefix, but they still follow the pattern of using **het** for forming the past tense.

## Negative Sentences in the Past Tense

To make a sentence negative in the past tense, you need to use the word **nie** (pronounced: nee) twice—just like you do in the present tense. You place **nie** after the verb and at the end of the sentence. Here are some examples:

- **Ek het nie gelees nie** (pronounced: ek het nee khuh-lees nee) – This means "I did not read."

- **Ons het nie gesing nie** (pronounced: ohns het nee khuh-sing nee) – This means "We did not sing."

- **Sy het nie gewerk nie** (pronounced: say het nee khuh-verk nee) – This means "She did not work."

As you can see, the negative form in the past tense is very similar to the present tense. You simply add **nie** twice to make the sentence negative.

## Asking Questions in the Past Tense

Asking questions in the past tense in Afrikaans is also simple. You can form questions by changing the word order or by using question words. Here are some examples:

- **Het jy die boek gelees?** (pronounced: het yay dee book khuh-lees) – This means "Did you read the book?"

- **Wat het jy gedoen?** (pronounced: vaht het yay khuh-doon) – This means "What did you do?"

- **Waar was jy?** (pronounced: vahr vahs yay) – This means "Where were you?"

Just like in English, you can use question words like **wat** (what), **waar** (where), and **wanneer** (when) to ask questions about past events. The word **het** is used to ask yes/no questions.

## Common Verbs in the Past Tense

Let's review some common verbs and their past tense forms in Afrikaans. These verbs are used often in daily conversations:

- **doen** (to do) becomes **gedoen** (did)

- **kyk** (to watch) becomes **gekyk** (watched)
- **speel** (to play) becomes **gespeel** (played)
- **werk** (to work) becomes **gewerk** (worked)
- **lees** (to read) becomes **gelees** (read)

Here are some example sentences using these verbs in the past tense:

- **Ek het my werk gedoen** (pronounced: ek het may verk khuh-doon) – This means "I did my work."
- **Sy het 'n fliek gekyk** (pronounced: say het uh fleek khuh-kayk) – This means "She watched a movie."
- **Ons het in die park gespeel** (pronounced: ohns het in dee park khuh-speel) – This means "We played in the park."

By learning these common verbs, you'll be able to talk about a wide range of past actions in Afrikaans.

## Key Points to Remember

- **Use "het" and add "ge-" to the verb**: To form the past tense in Afrikaans, use **het** and add **ge-** to the verb, like **Ek het gespeel** ("I played").
- **Irregular verbs don't use "ge-"**: Some verbs, like **was** ("was") and **het gehad** ("had"), do not follow the regular pattern.
- **Negative sentences use "nie" twice**: To make a sentence negative in the past tense, use **nie** after the verb and at the end of the sentence, like **Ek het nie gelees nie** ("I did not read").
- **Questions use "het"**: To ask questions in the past tense, use **het**, like **Het jy gespeel?** ("Did you play?").
- **Common past tense verbs**: Learn verbs like **gekyk** (watched), **gespeel** (played), and **gelees** (read) to describe actions that happened in the past.

# Chapter 29

# The Future Tense: Talking About What Will Happen

The future tense is used to talk about actions or events that have not happened yet but will happen at a later time. In Afrikaans, the future tense is simple to form and easy to use. Just like in English, we can use the future tense to describe things we plan to do, things we think will happen, or events that are scheduled to take place. In this chapter, we will learn how to form the future tense in Afrikaans and look at some examples to help you talk about the future with confidence.

## Forming the Future Tense

In Afrikaans, the future tense is formed using the word **sal** (pronounced: sul), which means "will." This is very similar to the way we form the future tense in English. You simply add **sal** before the verb to show that the action will happen in the future. Let's start with an example:

- **Ek sal speel** (pronounced: ek sul speel) – This means "I will play."

In this sentence, **sal** indicates that the action of playing will happen in the future. The basic structure for future tense sentences in Afrikaans is:

**[Subject] + sal + [verb]**

Let's look at some more examples:

- **Ek sal lees** (pronounced: ek sul lees) – This means "I will read."

- **Hy sal drink** (pronounced: hay sul drink) – This means "He will drink."

- **Sy sal werk** (pronounced: say sul verk) – This means "She will work."

- **Ons sal speel** (pronounced: ohns sul speel) – This means "We will play."

As you can see, the verb stays the same for all subjects (I, you, he, she, we, they), and only the word **sal** is added before the verb to indicate that the action will take place in the future.

## Using Verbs in the Future Tense

Now that we know how to form the future tense, let's look at how we can use it in sentences to talk about things that will happen. Here are some examples:

- **Ek sal my huiswerk doen** (pronounced: ek sul may hays-verk doon) – This means "I will do my homework."

- **Sy sal 'n boek lees** (pronounced: say sul uh book lees) – This means "She will read a book."

- **Ons sal later televisie kyk** (pronounced: ohns sul lah-ter tel-uh-vee-zee kayk) – This means "We will watch television later."

In each of these sentences, the verb is in the future tense, and the action will happen later. This is how you describe future events in Afrikaans using the basic **sal** + [verb] structure.

## Talking About Plans and Predictions

The future tense in Afrikaans is also used to talk about plans and predictions. Whether you are planning to do something or predicting that something will happen, you use **sal** to describe the action. Here are some examples:

- **Ek sal jou more sien** (pronounced: ek sul yow moh-ruh seen) – This means "I will see you tomorrow."

- **Dit sal reën** (pronounced: dit sul rayn) – This means "It will rain."

- **Ons sal volgende week sokker speel** (pronounced: ohns sul fol-ghen-duh veek soh-ker speel) – This means "We will play soccer next week."

Whether it's a plan for tomorrow or a prediction about the weather, **sal** helps you express what will happen in the future.

## Negative Sentences in the Future Tense

To make a sentence negative in the future tense, you need to use the word **nie** (pronounced: nee) twice—just like in the present and past tenses. You place **nie** after the verb and at the end of the sentence. Here are some examples:

- **Ek sal nie skool toe gaan nie** (pronounced: ek sul nee skohl too khaan nee) – This means "I will not go to school."

- **Sy sal nie sokker speel nie** (pronounced: say sul nee soh-ker speel nee) – This means "She will not play soccer."

- **Ons sal nie die fliek kyk nie** (pronounced: ohns sul nee dee fleek kayk nee) – This means "We will not watch the movie."

In these negative sentences, the word **nie** is used twice to show that the action will not happen in the future.

## Asking Questions in the Future Tense

In Afrikaans, asking questions in the future tense is simple. You can form questions by changing the word order or by using question words. Here are some examples:

- **Sal jy die boek lees?** (pronounced: sul yay dee book lees) – This means "Will you read the book?"

- **Wat sal jy doen?** (pronounced: vaht sul yay doon) – This means "What will you do?"

- **Waar sal ons gaan?** (pronounced: vahr sul ohns khaan) – This means "Where will we go?"

To ask yes/no questions, you simply put **sal** at the beginning of the sentence. For questions with words like **wat** (what) and **waar** (where), you place the question word at the beginning of the sentence.

## Common Verbs in the Future Tense

Let's review some common verbs and their future tense forms in Afrikaans. These verbs are used often in daily conversations and will help you talk about future actions:

- **doen** (to do) becomes **sal doen** (will do)

- **kyk** (to watch) becomes **sal kyk** (will watch)

- **speel** (to play) becomes **sal speel** (will play)

- **werk** (to work) becomes **sal werk** (will work)

- **lees** (to read) becomes **sal lees** (will read)

Here are some example sentences using these verbs in the future tense:

- **Ek sal my werk doen** (pronounced: ek sul may verk doon) – This means "I will do my work."

- **Sy sal 'n fliek kyk** (pronounced: say sul uh fleek kayk) – This means "She will watch a movie."

- **Ons sal sokker speel** (pronounced: ohns sul soh-ker speel) – This means "We will play soccer."

These common verbs will help you talk about many different actions in the future.

## Key Points to Remember

- **Use "sal" to form the future tense**: To talk about future actions in Afrikaans, use **sal** before the verb, like **Ek sal lees** ("I will read").

- **Plans and predictions**: You can use the future tense to talk about plans and predictions, such as **Ek sal jou sien** ("I will see you") or **Dit sal reën** ("It will rain").

- **Negative sentences use "nie" twice**: To make a sentence negative in the future tense, use **nie** after the verb and at the end of the sentence, like **Ek sal nie gaan nie** ("I will not go").

- **Questions use "sal"**: To ask questions in the future tense, start with **sal**, like **Sal jy lees?** ("Will you read ?").

- **Common future tense verbs**: Learn verbs like **sal doen** (will do), **sal kyk** (will watch), and **sal speel** (will play) to describe future actions.

# Chapter 30

# Reflexive Verbs: Actions We Do to Ourselves

Reflexive verbs are verbs that describe actions we do to ourselves. In English, we use reflexive pronouns like "myself" or "yourself" to show that we are performing an action on ourselves. For example, in the sentence "I wash myself," the verb **wash** is reflexive because it shows that the action is happening to the person doing it. In Afrikaans, reflexive verbs work in a similar way, but there are some differences in how we form these sentences.

## What Are Reflexive Verbs?

Reflexive verbs describe actions where the subject (the person doing the action) and the object (the person receiving the action) are the same. In Afrikaans, reflexive verbs are often used with reflexive pronouns like **myself** (myself) or **jouself** (yourself). These pronouns show that the action is being done to the person who is performing the action.

Let's start with a simple example:

- **Ek was myself** (pronounced: ek vahs my-selv) – This means "I wash myself."

In this sentence, the verb **was** (wash) is reflexive because the action is happening to the person performing it (myself). The reflexive pronoun **myself** makes it clear that the action is being done to the same person.

## Using Reflexive Pronouns

To form reflexive verbs in Afrikaans, you need to use reflexive pronouns. These pronouns change depending on the subject of the sentence. Here are the most common reflexive pronouns in Afrikaans:

- **myself** (pronounced: my-selv) – This means "myself."

- **jouself** (pronounced: yow-selv) – This means "yourself" (singular).

- **homself** (pronounced: hom-selv) – This means "himself."

- **haarself** (pronounced: hahr-selv) – This means "herself."

- **onselves** (pronounced: ohn-selv) – This means "ourselves."

- **hulleself** (pronounced: huh-luh-selv) – This means "themselves."

These reflexive pronouns are used to show that the action is being done by and to the same person. Let's look at some more examples of reflexive verbs using different pronouns:

- **Ek sny myself** (pronounced: ek snay my-selv) – This means "I cut myself."

- **Jy trek jouself aan** (pronounced: yay trek yow-selv ahn) – This means "You dress yourself."

- **Hy skeer homself** (pronounced: hay skeer hom-selv) – This means "He shaves himself."

- **Sy kyk na haarself in die spieël** (pronounced: say kayk nah hahr-selv in dee spee-uhl) – This means "She looks at herself in the mirror."

- **Ons help onsself** (pronounced: ohns help ohn-selv) – This means "We help ourselves."

In each of these examples, the reflexive pronoun is used to show that the subject is performing the action on themselves.

## Common Reflexive Verbs

In Afrikaans, there are many reflexive verbs that you will use in everyday conversations. Here are some common reflexive verbs and their meanings:

- **was** (pronounced: vahs) – This means "to wash."

- **sny** (pronounced: snay) – This means "to cut."

- **trek aan** (pronounced: trek ahn) – This means "to dress" (or "to put on clothes").

- **skeer** (pronounced: skeer) – This means "to shave."

- **help** (pronounced: help) – This means "to help."

Here are some example sentences using these common reflexive verbs:

- **Ek was myself elke oggend** (pronounced: ek vahs my-selv el-kuh oh-ghond) – This means "I wash myself every morning."

- **Hy skeer homself elke dag** (pronounced: hay skeer hom-selv el-kuh dahkh) – This means "He shaves himself every day."

- **Ons trek onsself vinnig aan** (pronounced: ohns trek ohn-selv fin-nikh ahn) – This means "We dress ourselves quickly."

By learning these reflexive verbs, you'll be able to talk about many actions you do to yourself in Afrikaans.

## Negative Sentences with Reflexive Verbs

To make a sentence with a reflexive verb negative in Afrikaans, you need to add the word **nie** twice—just like in other tenses. You place **nie** after the verb and at the end of the sentence. Here are some examples:

- **Ek sny nie myself nie** (pronounced: ek snay nee my-selv nee) – This means "I do not cut myself."

- **Jy was nie jouself nie** (pronounced: yay vahs nee yow-selv nee) – This means "You do not wash yourself."

- **Sy trek nie haarself aan nie** (pronounced: say trek nee hahr-selv ahn nee) – This means "She does not dress herself."

In each of these sentences, the word **nie** is used twice to turn the sentence into a negative. This is the same structure we use for other negative sentences in Afrikaans.

## Asking Questions with Reflexive Verbs

Asking questions with reflexive verbs in Afrikaans is simple. You can form questions by changing the word order or by using question words. Here are some examples:

- **Was jy jouself?** (pronounced: vahs yay yow-selv) – This means "Did you wash yourself?"

- **Trek hy homself aan?** (pronounced: trek hay hom-selv ahn) – This means "Does he dress himself?"

- **Hoe help jy jouself?** (pronounced: hoo help yay yow-selv) – This means "How do you help yourself?"

Just like with other questions in Afrikaans, you can use **wat** (what), **waar** (where), **hoe** (how), and other question words to ask about reflexive actions.

## Combining Reflexive Verbs with Other Words

In Afrikaans, you can also combine reflexive verbs with other words to create more complex sentences. For example, you can add adverbs of time, place, or manner to give more information about the action. Here are some examples:

- **Ek was myself vinnig** (pronounced: ek vahs my-selv fin-nikh) – This means "I wash myself quickly."

- **Sy sny haarself elke dag** (pronounced: say snay hahr-selv el-kuh dahkh) – This means "She cuts herself every day."

- **Ons trek onsself warm klere aan** (pronounced: ohns trek ohn-selv var-uhm klee-ruh ahn) – This means "We put on warm clothes."

By combining reflexive verbs with other words, you can make your sentences more detailed and descriptive.

## Key Points to Remember

- **Reflexive verbs show actions done to oneself**: Reflexive verbs are used when the subject and object are the same, such as **Ek was myself** ("I wash myself").

- **Use reflexive pronouns**: Reflexive pronouns like **myself** (myself) and **jouself** (yourself) are used to show that the action is happening to the person performing it.

- **Common reflexive verbs**: Learn verbs like **was** (wash), **sny** (cut), and **trek aan** (dress) to talk about actions you do to yourself.

- **Negative sentences use "nie" twice**: To make a reflexive sentence negative, use **nie** after the verb and at the end of the sentence, like **Ek sny nie myself nie** ("I do not cut myself").

- **Ask questions with reflexive verbs**: Use reflexive verbs in questions by changing the word order, like **Was jy jouself?** ("Did you wash yourself?").

# Chapter 31

# Irregular Verbs and Their Usage

In any language, some verbs follow predictable rules when you change their form, while others don't. These verbs are called "irregular verbs." In Afrikaans, irregular verbs are verbs that do not follow the usual patterns when forming the past tense, future tense, or other forms. Even though they are irregular, many of these verbs are very common in everyday conversation. In this chapter, we will explore some of the most important irregular verbs in Afrikaans and how to use them correctly in sentences.

## What Are Irregular Verbs?

Irregular verbs are verbs that don't follow the regular rules for conjugation. For example, in English, the verb "go" becomes "went" in the past tense instead of "goed." In Afrikaans, irregular verbs also change in ways that don't follow the regular patterns. These verbs are important to learn because they are used frequently in everyday speech and writing.

## Irregular Verb: "Wees" (To Be)

One of the most important irregular verbs in Afrikaans is **wees** (pronounced: vees), which means "to be." This verb is irregular because it changes form in different tenses. Here's how you use **wees** in different tenses:

- **Present tense: is** (pronounced: is) – This means "am," "is," or "are." For example: **Ek is bly** (pronounced: ek is blay) – This means "I am happy."

- **Past tense: was** (pronounced: vahs) – This means "was" or "were." For example: **Hy was siek** (pronounced: hay vahs seek) – This means "He was sick."

- **Future tense: sal wees** (pronounced: sul vees) – This means "will be." For example: **Sy sal bly wees** (pronounced: say sul blay vees) – This means "She will be happy."

As you can see, **wees** changes its form depending on the tense. It's important to remember these different forms because they are used often in everyday conversation.

## Irregular Verb: "Hê" (To Have)

Another important irregular verb is **hê** (pronounced: heh), which means "to have." This verb also changes form in the past tense. Here's how you use **hê** in different tenses:

- **Present tense: het** (pronounced: het) – This means "have" or "has." For example: **Ek het 'n boek** (pronounced: ek het uh book) – This means "I have a book."

- **Past tense: het gehad** (pronounced: het khuh-haht) – This means "had." For example: **Ons het 'n hond gehad** (pronounced: ohns het uh hond khuh-haht) – This means "We had a dog."

- **Future tense: sal hê** (pronounced: sul heh) – This means "will have." For example: **Jy sal 'n kans hê** (pronounced: yay sul uh kahns heh) – This means "You will have a chance."

Notice how **hê** becomes **het gehad** in the past tense. This is an example of how irregular verbs don't always follow predictable rules.

## Irregular Verb: "Gaan" (To Go)

The verb **gaan** (pronounced: khahn), which means "to go," is another commonly used irregular verb in Afrikaans. Here's how you use **gaan** in different tenses:

- **Present tense: gaan** – This means "go" or "goes." For example: **Ek gaan na die winkel** (pronounced: ek khahn nah dee vink-uhl) – This means "I am going to the store."

- **Past tense: het gegaan** (pronounced: het khuh-khahn) – This means "went." For example: **Hy het huis toe gegaan** (pronounced: hay het hays too khuh-khahn) – This means "He went home."

- **Future tense: sal gaan** – This means "will go." For example: **Ons sal volgende week gaan** (pronounced: ohns sul fol-ghen-duh veek khahn) – This means "We will go next week."

As you can see, **gaan** stays the same in the present and future tenses, but in the past tense, it becomes **het gegaan**.

## Irregular Verb: "Kom" (To Come)

The verb **kom** (pronounced: kohm), which means "to come," is another irregular verb that changes form in different tenses. Here's how you use **kom** in sentences:

- **Present tense: kom** – This means "come" or "comes." For example: **Sy kom huis toe** (pronounced: say kohm hays too) – This means "She is coming home."

- **Past tense: het gekom** (pronounced: het khuh-kohm) – This means "came." For example: **Ek het na die partytjie gekom** (pronounced: ek het nah dee par-tay-kee khuh-kohm) – This means "I came to the party."

- **Future tense: sal kom** – This means "will come." For example: **Hulle sal later kom** (pronounced: huh-luh sul lah-ter kohm) – This means "They will come later."

Like other irregular verbs, **kom** changes in the past tense, becoming **het gekom**.

## Irregular Verb: "Doen" (To Do)

Another important irregular verb is **doen** (pronounced: doon), which means "to do." Here's how you use **doen** in different tenses:

- **Present tense: doen** – This means "do" or "does." For example: **Ek doen my huiswerk** (pronounced: ek doon may hays-verk) – This means "I do my homework."

- **Past tense: het gedoen** (pronounced: het khuh-doon) – This means "did." For example: **Sy het haar werk gedoen** (pronounced: say het hahr verk khuh-doon) – This means "She did her work."

- **Future tense: sal doen** – This means "will do." For example: **Hy sal dit môre doen** (pronounced: hay sul dit moh-ruh doon) – This means "He will do it tomorrow."

In the past tense, **doen** becomes **het gedoen**, another example of how irregular verbs in Afrikaans change form.

## Negative Sentences with Irregular Verbs

When you use irregular verbs in negative sentences, you need to add the word **nie** twice, just like with regular verbs. Here are some examples:

- **Ek is nie siek nie** (pronounced: ek is nee seek nee) – This means "I am not sick."

- **Hy het nie gegaan nie** (pronounced: hay het nee khuh-khahn nee) – This means "He did not go."

- **Sy sal nie kom nie** (pronounced: say sul nee kohm nee) – This means "She will not come."

Even though the verb is irregular, the rules for making negative sentences stay the same.

Asking Questions with Irregular Verbs

To ask questions with irregular verbs, you can simply change the word order or use question words like **wat** (what), **wanneer** (when), or **waar** (where). Here are some examples:

- **Is jy siek?** (pronounced: is yay seek) – This means "Are you sick?"

- **Het jy na die skool gegaan?** (pronounced: het yay nah dee skohl khuh-khahn) – This means "Did you go to the school?"

- **Sal hy môre kom?** (pronounced: sul hay moh-ruh kohm) – This means "Will he come tomorrow?"

Asking questions with irregular verbs follows the same rules as asking questions with regular verbs.

## Key Points to Remember

- **Irregular verbs don't follow regular patterns**: Irregular verbs, like **wees** (to be) and **hê** (to have), change in unpredictable ways, especially in the past tense.

- **Common irregular verbs**: Important irregular verbs include **wees** (to be), **hê** (to have), **gaan** (to go), **kom** (to come), and **doen** (to do).

- **Use "nie" for negative sentences**: To make negative sentences with irregular verbs, use **nie** after the verb and again at the end of the sentence.

- **Asking questions with irregular verbs**: You can ask questions by changing the word order or using question words, just like with regular verbs.

- **Past tense forms of irregular verbs**: Many irregular verbs have special past tense forms, like **het gegaan** (went) or **het gehad** (had).

# Chapter 32

# Talking About Travel and Directions

When you are in a new place, knowing how to talk about travel and directions is very important. In Afrikaans, there are specific words and phrases you can use to talk about how to get from one place to another, how to ask for directions, and how to give directions. In this chapter, we will go over some basic travel vocabulary, common phrases for asking and giving directions, and examples to help you understand how to use these in conversations.

## Common Travel Vocabulary

Before we start talking about directions, it's helpful to know some common words related to travel. Here are a few key words you'll need:

- **Reis** (pronounced: rays) – This means "travel."

- **Vlieg** (pronounced: fleegh) – This means "fly."

- **Trein** (pronounced: trayn) – This means "train."

- **Bus** (pronounced: bus) – This means "bus."

- **Kar** (pronounced: kahr) – This means "car."

- **Pad** (pronounced: paht) – This means "road."

- **Vlug** (pronounced: flugh) – This means "flight."

- **Stasie** (pronounced: stah-see) – This means "station."

- **Lughawe** (pronounced: lug-hah-wuh) – This means "airport."

These words will help you talk about different modes of transportation, whether you're traveling by car, train, bus, or plane.

## Asking for Directions

When you're in an unfamiliar place, you'll probably need to ask someone for directions. In Afrikaans, you can ask for directions using some simple phrases. Here are a few examples:

- **Waar is die...** (pronounced: vahr is dee...) – This means "Where is the...?" You can use this to ask for the location of something. For example: **Waar is die stasie?** (Where is the station?)

- **Hoe kom ek by...** (pronounced: hoo kohm ek bay...) – This means "How do I get to...?" For example: **Hoe kom ek by die lughawe?** (How do I get to the airport?)

- **Kan jy my help?** (pronounced: kahn yay may help) – This means "Can you help me?"

These simple phrases will help you start a conversation when you need help finding your way. Don't forget to use the polite word **asseblief** (pronounced: ah-suh-bleef), which means "please." For example: **Waar is die lughawe, asseblief?** (Where is the airport, please?)

## Giving Directions

If someone asks you for directions, it's important to know how to respond. Here are some common phrases you can use to give directions in Afrikaans:

- **Gaan reguit** (pronounced: khahn rekh-ayt) – This means "Go straight."

- **Draai links** (pronounced: drah-ee links) – This means "Turn left."

- **Draai regs** (pronounced: drah-ee rekhs) – This means "Turn right."

- **By die stopstraat** (pronounced: bay dee stop-straht) – This means "At the stop street."

- **Om die hoek** (pronounced: om dee hook) – This means "Around the corner."

- **Oorkant** (pronounced: oor-kahnt) – This means "Across" or "opposite."

Let's look at some examples of how to use these phrases:

- **Gaan reguit en draai links by die stopstraat** (pronounced: khahn rekh-ayt en drah-ee links bay dee stop-straht) – This means "Go straight and turn left at the stop street."

- **Draai regs by die kruising** (pronounced: drah-ee rekhs bay dee kroy-sing) – This means "Turn right at the intersection."
- **Die lughawe is oorkant die pad** (pronounced: dee lug-hah-wuh is oor-kahnt dee paht) – This means "The airport is across the road."

These phrases will help you give clear directions to others. When giving directions, be sure to use landmarks or street names to make your instructions easier to follow.

## Describing Locations

When you are traveling, you might need to describe where something is located. Here are some useful words for talking about locations in Afrikaans:

- **naby** (pronounced: nah-bay) – This means "near."
- **ver** (pronounced: fehr) – This means "far."
- **langs** (pronounced: lahngs) – This means "next to."
- **voor** (pronounced: fohr) – This means "in front of."
- **agter** (pronounced: ahkh-ter) – This means "behind."
- **tussen** (pronounced: tuh-sen) – This means "between."

Here are some example sentences using these words:

- **Die stasie is naby** (pronounced: dee stah-see is nah-bay) – This means "The station is near."
- **Die lughawe is ver** (pronounced: dee lug-hah-wuh is fehr) – This means "The airport is far."
- **Die hotel is langs die park** (pronounced: dee hoh-tel is lahngs dee park) – This means "The hotel is next to the park."

These words will help you describe the location of places when you're giving directions or talking about where something is.

## Talking About Different Modes of Transportation

When traveling, it's also important to know how to talk about different ways to get around. Here are some useful phrases for talking about transportation in Afrikaans:

- **Ek ry met die bus** (pronounced: ek ray met dee bus) – This means "I am taking the bus."

- **Ek vlieg na Johannesburg** (pronounced: ek fleegh nah yo-han-uhs-burg) – This means "I am flying to Johannesburg."

- **Ons ry met die trein** (pronounced: ohns ray met dee trayn) – This means "We are taking the train."

You can use the word **ry** (pronounced: ray) to talk about riding in a car, bus, or train, and **vlieg** to talk about flying on a plane. These phrases will help you explain how you are traveling from one place to another.

## Common Travel Questions

Here are some common questions you might ask or hear when traveling:

- **Hoe laat vertrek die trein?** (pronounced: hoo laht fer-trek dee trayn) – This means "What time does the train leave?"

- **Waar koop ek 'n kaartjie?** (pronounced: vahr kohp ek uh kahrt-kee) – This means "Where do I buy a ticket?"

- **Hoe lank neem dit om daar te kom?** (pronounced: hoo lahng neem dit om dahr tuh kohm) – This means "How long does it take to get there?"

Knowing these questions will help you when you're at a station or airport and need information about your travel plans.

## Key Points to Remember

- **Common travel vocabulary**: Words like **reis** (travel), **vlieg** (fly), and **kar** (car) will help you talk about different modes of transportation.

- **Asking for directions**: Use phrases like **Waar is die...?** (Where is the...?) and **Hoe kom ek by...?** (How do I get to...?) to ask for directions.

- **Giving directions**: Use phrases like **Gaan reguit** (Go straight), **Draai links** (Turn left), and **Oorkant** (Across) to give directions.

- **Describing locations**: Words like **naby** (near), **langs** (next to), and **agter** (behind) will help you describe where something is.

- **Talking about transportation**: Use phrases like **Ek ry met die bus** (I am taking the bus) and **Ek vlieg** (I am flying) to describe how you are traveling.

# Chapter 33

# Health and Medical Vocabulary

Talking about health and medical topics is important in any language. Whether you're feeling sick or just need to go to the doctor, knowing how to describe your symptoms and talk about health is essential. In this chapter, we will go over some basic health and medical vocabulary in Afrikaans. We'll cover words and phrases you can use to describe how you're feeling, common illnesses, and how to communicate with a doctor or nurse.

## Common Health Vocabulary

To start, here are some common words related to health and the body in Afrikaans:

- **Liggaam** (pronounced: lig-gahm) – This means "body."

- **Kop** (pronounced: kohp) – This means "head."

- **Hart** (pronounced: hart) – This means "heart."

- **Oë** (pronounced: uh) – This means "eyes."

- **Oor** (pronounced: oor) – This means "ear."

- **Mond** (pronounced: mond) – This means "mouth."

- **Maag** (pronounced: mahg) – This means "stomach."

- **Hand** (pronounced: hahnd) – This means "hand."

- **Voet** (pronounced: foot) – This means "foot."

These words will help you describe different parts of the body, which is important when talking about health or medical issues.

## Describing Symptoms

When you're not feeling well, it's important to know how to describe your symptoms. Here are some common words and phrases you can use to talk about how you're feeling:

- **Ek voel siek** (pronounced: ek fool seek) – This means "I feel sick."

- **Ek het pyn** (pronounced: ek het payn) – This means "I have pain."

- **My maag is seer** (pronounced: may mahg is seer) – This means "My stomach hurts."

- **Ek het 'n hoofpyn** (pronounced: ek het uh hohf-payn) – This means "I have a headache."

- **My keel is seer** (pronounced: may keel is seer) – This means "My throat is sore."

- **Ek is naar** (pronounced: ek is nah-r) – This means "I feel nauseous."

These phrases will help you explain how you're feeling to a doctor, nurse, or pharmacist. Whether you have a sore throat or a stomachache, knowing how to describe your symptoms is very important when seeking medical help.

## Common Illnesses

Here are some common illnesses and conditions that you might need to talk about in Afrikaans:

- **Griep** (pronounced: greep) – This means "flu."

- **Verkoue** (pronounced: fer-koh-uh) – This means "cold" (as in the common cold).

- **Koors** (pronounced: koors) – This means "fever."

- **Infeksie** (pronounced: in-fek-see) – This means "infection."

- **Allergie** (pronounced: ah-lair-ghee) – This means "allergy."

- **Infeksie** (pronounced: in-fek-see) – This means "infection."

Here are some example sentences using these words:

- **Ek het griep** (pronounced: ek het greep) – This means "I have the flu."

- **Sy het 'n verkoue** (pronounced: say het uh fer-koh-uh) – This means "She has a cold."

- **Ek het 'n koors** (pronounced: ek het uh koors) – This means "I have a fever."

These words will help you talk about common illnesses when you're not feeling well or when you need to explain what's wrong to a doctor.

## Talking to a Doctor

When visiting a doctor, there are certain phrases you can use to explain what's wrong and to ask questions. Here are some useful phrases:

- **Ek moet 'n dokter sien** (pronounced: ek moot uh dok-ter seen) – This means "I need to see a doctor."

- **Ek voel nie lekker nie** (pronounced: ek fool nee lek-ker nee) – This means "I don't feel well."

- **Wat is verkeerd?** (pronounced: vaht is fer-kayrt) – This means "What is wrong?"

- **Ek het hierdie simptome** (pronounced: ek het hee-deer-ree simp-toh-muh) – This means "I have these symptoms."

- **Hoe lank sal ek siek wees?** (pronounced: hoo lahng sul ek seek vees) – This means "How long will I be sick?"

These phrases will help you explain your condition to a doctor and ask about what's wrong or how long it will take to feel better.

## Talking About Injuries

Sometimes, you might need to talk about injuries, like a broken arm or a cut. Here are some useful words and phrases for describing injuries in Afrikaans:

- **Ek het my arm gebreek** (pronounced: ek het may arm khuh-breek) – This means "I broke my arm."

- **Ek het my enkel seergemaak** (pronounced: ek het may ayn-kuhl seer-ghuh-mahk) – This means "I hurt my ankle."

- **Ek het 'n sny** (pronounced: ek het uh snay) – This means "I have a cut."

- **Ek bloei** (pronounced: ek bloo-ee) – This means "I am bleeding."

Knowing how to describe an injury will help you explain what happened if you need medical attention.

## At the Pharmacy

When you need medicine, you might have to go to the pharmacy. Here are some words and phrases you can use when asking for medicine or advice at a pharmacy in Afrikaans:

- **Apteek** (pronounced: ahp-teek) – This means "pharmacy."

- **Medisyne** (pronounced: meh-dee-say-nuh) – This means "medicine."

- **Ek benodig medisyne** (pronounced: ek beh-noh-dig meh-dee-say-nuh) – This means "I need medicine."

- **Ek het 'n voorskrif** (pronounced: ek het uh foor-skrif) – This means "I have a prescription."

These phrases will help you when you need to visit a pharmacy to get medicine or fill a prescription.

## Key Points to Remember

- **Common health vocabulary**: Words like **liggaam** (body), **kop** (head), and **maag** (stomach) will help you talk about different parts of the body.

- **Describing symptoms**: Use phrases like **Ek voel siek** (I feel sick) and **My maag is seer** (My stomach hurts) to describe how you're feeling.

- **Talking to a doctor**: Phrases like **Ek moet 'n dokter sien** (I need to see a doctor) and **Wat is verkeerd?** (What is wrong?) will help you communicate with a doctor.

- **Talking about injuries**: Use phrases like **Ek het my arm gebreek** (I broke my arm) or **Ek het 'n sny** (I have a cut) to describe injuries.

- **At the pharmacy**: Words like **apteek** (pharmacy) and **medisyne** (medicine) will help you when you need to get medicine or fill a prescription.

# Chapter 34

# Shopping and Bargaining: Phrases and Terms

Shopping is a fun and practical way to learn a new language. Whether you're buying clothes, food, or souvenirs, knowing how to ask for what you want, talk about prices, and even bargain can be very useful. In this chapter, we will explore some important phrases and terms related to shopping and bargaining in Afrikaans. You'll learn how to ask for prices, negotiate a deal, and talk about different items in the store.

## Common Shopping Vocabulary

Before you start shopping, it's helpful to know some basic words related to stores, products, and money. Here are a few key words you'll need:

- **Winkel** (pronounced: vink-uhl) – This means "store" or "shop."

- **Mark** (pronounced: mark) – This means "market."

- **Produk** (pronounced: pro-duhk) – This means "product."

- **Prys** (pronounced: prays) – This means "price."

- **Kontant** (pronounced: kon-tahnt) – This means "cash."

- **Kredietkaart** (pronounced: kreh-dee-et-kahrt) – This means "credit card."

These words will help you navigate stores, markets, and other shopping places. Let's now explore how to use these words in sentences and conversations.

## Asking About Prices

One of the first things you'll want to ask when shopping is the price of an item. Here are some useful phrases to ask about prices in Afrikaans:

- **Hoeveel kos dit?** (pronounced: hoo-feel kohs dit) – This means "How much does this cost?"

- **Wat is die prys?** (pronounced: vaht is dee prays) – This means "What is the price?"

- **Hoe duur is dit?** (pronounced: hoo deur is dit) – This means "How expensive is it?"

You can use these phrases to ask for the price of items, whether you're in a store or at a market. If you're pointing to something specific, you can use the phrase **Hoeveel kos hierdie?** (pronounced: hoo-feel kohs heer-dee), which means "How much does this cost?"

## Talking About Payment

Once you know the price, you'll need to talk about how you want to pay. Here are some useful phrases related to payment:

- **Ek wil dit koop** (pronounced: ek vil dit kohp) – This means "I want to buy this."

- **Ek betaal met kontant** (pronounced: ek beh-tahl met kon-tahnt) – This means "I'll pay with cash."

- **Ek betaal met 'n kredietkaart** (pronounced: ek beh-tahl met uh kreh-dee-et-kahrt) – This means "I'll pay with a credit card."

- **Kan ek asseblief met kontant betaal?** (pronounced: kahn ek ah-suh-bleef met kon-tahnt beh-tahl) – This means "Can I please pay with cash?"

It's important to know how you plan to pay before you get to the register. If you're using cash, you can say **kontant**, and if you're using a card, you can say **kredietkaart**.

## Bargaining and Negotiating

In some places, especially at markets, you might want to negotiate the price of an item. Here are some phrases you can use to bargain in Afrikaans:

- **Kan jy die prys laer maak?** (pronounced: kahn yay dee prays lah-er mahk) – This means "Can you lower the price?"

- **Is daar afslag?** (pronounced: is dahr ahf-slakh) – This means "Is there a discount?"

- **Dit is te duur** (pronounced: dit is tuh deur) – This means "It is too expensive."

- **Ek het nie genoeg geld nie** (pronounced: ek het nee ghuh-noekh khelt nee) – This means "I don't have enough money."

When bargaining, it's important to be polite and friendly. You can add **asseblief** (please) to any request to make it sound more polite. For example, you could say **Kan jy asseblief die prys laer maak?** (Can you please lower the price?).

## Describing Items You Want to Buy

Sometimes, you might want to describe the item you're looking for. Here are some useful words to describe items when shopping:

- **Groot** (pronounced: khroot) – This means "big" or "large."

- **Klein** (pronounced: klayn) – This means "small."

- **Goedkoop** (pronounced: khoot-kohp) – This means "cheap" or "inexpensive."

- **Deur** (pronounced: deur) – This means "expensive."

- **Mooi** (pronounced: moy) – This means "beautiful."

- **Nuut** (pronounced: noot) – This means "new."

- **Oud** (pronounced: owt) – This means "old."

Here are some example sentences using these words:

- **Ek soek 'n groot hemp** (pronounced: ek sook uh khroot hemp) – This means "I'm looking for a large shirt."

- **Hierdie broek is goedkoop** (pronounced: heer-dee brook is khoot-kohp) – This means "These pants are cheap."

- **Ek wil 'n nuwe skoene hê** (pronounced: ek vil uh noov-uh skooh-nuh heh) – This means "I want new shoes."

These words will help you describe what you're looking for when shopping, whether it's a large item, a new product, or something inexpensive.

## Talking About Quantity

When you're shopping, you might need to talk about how many or how much of something you want to buy. Here are some useful phrases to talk about quantity in Afrikaans:

- **Ek wil een hê** (pronounced: ek vil een heh) – This means "I want one."

- **Ek wil twee hê** (pronounced: ek vil twee heh) – This means "I want two."

- **Hoeveel is dit?** (pronounced: hoo-feel is dit) – This means "How many is it?" or "How much is it?"

- **Ek wil 'n paar hê** (pronounced: ek vil uh pahr heh) – This means "I want a few."

These phrases will help you talk about how many items you want to buy, whether you want just one item or a few.

## Asking for Help

Sometimes, you might need help finding something in a store. Here are some useful phrases for asking for help when shopping in Afrikaans:

- **Kan jy my help?** (pronounced: kahn yay may help) – This means "Can you help me?"

- **Waar is die klere?** (pronounced: vahr is dee klee-ruh) – This means "Where are the clothes?"

- **Waar is die skoene?** (pronounced: vahr is dee skooh-nuh) – This means "Where are the shoes?"

- **Ek soek 'n geskenk** (pronounced: ek sook uh ghe-skenk) – This means "I'm looking for a gift."

These phrases will help you ask for assistance if you can't find something in a store. It's always helpful to know how to ask for help when you're shopping.

## Key Points to Remember

- **Common shopping vocabulary**: Words like **winkel** (store), **prys** (price), and **kontant** (cash) will help you navigate shopping in Afrikaans.

- **Asking about prices**: Use phrases like **Hoeveel kos dit?** (How much does this cost?) and **Wat is die prys?** (What is the price?) to ask about the cost of items.

- **Talking about payment**: Use phrases like **Ek betaal met kontant** (I'll pay with cash) or **Ek betaal met 'n kredietkaart** (I'll pay with a credit card) to talk about how you'll pay.

- **Bargaining and negotiating**: Use phrases like **Kan jy die prys laer maak?** (Can you lower the price?) or **Is daar afslag?** (Is there a discount?) when bargaining.

- **Asking for help**: Phrases like **Kan jy my help?** (Can you help me?) and **Waar is die klere?** (Where are the clothes?) will help you ask for assistance in a store.

# Chapter 35

# Jobs and Professions: Talking About Work

Knowing how to talk about jobs and professions is an important part of learning any language. Whether you're describing what someone does for work or asking about their job, having the right vocabulary can help you have conversations about people's occupations. In Afrikaans, there are specific words and phrases used to describe different types of jobs and professions. In this chapter, we will cover common job titles, how to ask about work, and how to describe what people do for a living.

## Common Jobs and Professions

Let's start with some common jobs and professions in Afrikaans. Here are some words that you might hear when talking about different types of work:

- **Dokter** (pronounced: dok-ter) – This means "doctor."

- **Onderwyser** (pronounced: on-der-vay-ser) – This means "teacher."

- **Ingenieur** (pronounced: in-ghuh-neer) – This means "engineer."

- **Verpleegster** (pronounced: fer-pleegh-ster) – This means "nurse."

- **Rekenmeester** (pronounced: rey-ken-mees-ter) – This means "accountant."

- **Prokureur** (pronounced: pro-koo-reur) – This means "lawyer."

- **Polisieman** (pronounced: poo-lee-see-man) – This means "policeman."

- **Brandweerman** (pronounced: brunt-veer-man) – This means "firefighter."

- **Boer** (pronounced: boor) – This means "farmer."

- **Werktuigkundige** (pronounced: verk-taykh-kun-di-ghuh) – This means "mechanic."

These are just a few examples of the many professions people can have. It's helpful to learn job titles so you can ask about what people do or describe their work.

## Asking About Jobs

If you want to ask someone what their job is, there are a few different ways to ask the question in Afrikaans. Here are some common phrases you can use to ask about someone's profession:

- **Wat doen jy vir 'n lewe?** (pronounced: vaht doon yay fer uh lew-uh) – This means "What do you do for a living?"

- **Wat is jou beroep?** (pronounced: vaht is yow beh-roop) – This means "What is your profession?"

- **Waar werk jy?** (pronounced: vahr verk yay) – This means "Where do you work?"

You can use these phrases to ask about someone's job or workplace. If you want to be more specific, you can also ask **Wat doen jou ma of pa?** (pronounced: vaht doon yow mah or pah), which means "What does your mom or dad do?"

## Talking About Your Own Job

If someone asks you about your job, here are some ways you can respond and talk about what you do for work:

- **Ek is 'n onderwyser** (pronounced: ek is uh on-der-vay-ser) – This means "I am a teacher."

- **Ek werk by 'n hospitaal** (pronounced: ek verk bay uh hos-pee-taal) – This means "I work at a hospital."

- **Ek is 'n rekenmeester** (pronounced: ek is uh rey-ken-mees-ter) – This means "I am an accountant."

When describing your job, you can use the structure **Ek is 'n...** (I am a...) followed by your profession. If you work at a specific place, you can say **Ek werk by...** (I work at...) and name the place.

## Describing What People Do for Work

Sometimes, you might need to describe what someone else does for work. Here are some phrases to help you talk about what other people do for a living:

- **Hy is 'n dokter** (pronounced: hay is uh dok-ter) – This means "He is a doctor."

- **Sy is 'n verpleegster** (pronounced: say is uh fer-pleegh-ster) – This means "She is a nurse."

- **Hulle werk in 'n fabriek** (pronounced: huh-luh verk in uh fah-breek) – This means "They work in a factory."

You can use **Hy is 'n...** (He is a...) or **Sy is 'n...** (She is a...) to describe what someone does. If you're talking about where they work, you can use **Hulle werk by...** (They work at...) followed by the location.

## Talking About Future Jobs

Sometimes, you might want to talk about what you or someone else wants to do in the future. Here are some phrases for talking about future professions:

- **Ek wil 'n dokter word** (pronounced: ek vil uh dok-ter vohrt) – This means "I want to become a doctor."

- **Sy wil 'n onderwyser wees** (pronounced: say vil uh on-der-vay-ser vees) – This means "She wants to be a teacher."

- **Hy wil in die toekoms 'n ingenieur wees** (pronounced: hay vil in dee too-koms uh in-ghuh-neer vees) – This means "He wants to be an engineer in the future."

When talking about future jobs, you can use the phrase **Ek wil 'n...** (I want to be a...) followed by the job title. You can also talk about what other people want to do by using **Hy wil 'n...** (He wants to be a...) or **Sy wil 'n...** (She wants to be a...).

## Workplaces

Knowing where people work is just as important as knowing what they do. Here are some common words related to workplaces in Afrikaans:

- **Kantoor** (pronounced: kan-toor) – This means "office."

- **Hospitaal** (pronounced: hos-pee-taal) – This means "hospital."
- **Fabriek** (pronounced: fah-breek) – This means "factory."
- **Skool** (pronounced: skohl) – This means "school."
- **Winkel** (pronounced: vink-uhl) – This means "store" or "shop."
- **Polisiestasie** (pronounced: poo-lee-see-ah-stah-see) – This means "police station."

These words will help you talk about different places where people work. For example, if someone is a teacher, they might work at a **skool** (school), and if someone is a nurse, they might work at a **hospitaal** (hospital).

## Talking About Different Types of Jobs

There are different ways to talk about the type of job someone has. Here are a few phrases to describe different types of jobs:

- **Voltyds werk** (pronounced: fol-taits verk) – This means "full-time job."
- **Deeltyds werk** (pronounced: deel-taits verk) – This means "part-time job."
- **Vryskutwerk** (pronounced: fray-skoot-verk) – This means "freelance work."

If someone works a **voltyds werk**, it means they work full-time, while someone with a **deeltyds werk** works part-time. If someone works as a freelancer, they might do **vryskutwerk**.

## Key Points to Remember

- **Common jobs and professions**: Words like **dokter** (doctor), **onderwyser** (teacher), and **polisieman** (policeman) will help you talk about different jobs.
- **Asking about jobs**: Use phrases like **Wat doen jy vir 'n lewe?** (What do you do for a living?) or **Wat is jou beroep?** (What is your profession?) to ask about someone's job.
- **Talking about your own job**: Use the structure **Ek is 'n...** (I am a...) followed by your job title to describe what you do for work.
- **Describing workplaces**: Words like **kantoor** (office), **hospitaal** (hospital), and **skool** (school) will help you describe where people work.

- **Talking about future jobs**: Use the phrase **Ek wil 'n...** (I want to be a...) to talk about what you or others want to do for work in the future.

# Chapter 36

# Afrikaans Idioms and Sayings

Every language has idioms and sayings that are unique to its culture. Idioms are phrases or expressions that don't always mean what the words literally say. Instead, they have a special meaning understood by people who know the language well. In Afrikaans, there are many interesting idioms and sayings that can make your speech more colorful and fun. In this chapter, we will explore some of the most common Afrikaans idioms, explain what they mean, and show you how to use them in sentences.

## What Are Idioms?

An idiom is a phrase or expression with a meaning that is different from the literal meaning of the individual words. For example, in English, the phrase "it's raining cats and dogs" doesn't mean that animals are falling from the sky—it just means that it's raining heavily. In Afrikaans, there are many similar expressions that might sound funny or strange if you try to translate them word for word.

Let's take a look at some popular Afrikaans idioms and what they mean.

## Common Afrikaans Idioms and Their Meanings

### "Die bobbejaan agter die berg gaan haal"

**Literal meaning:** "Fetch the baboon from behind the mountain."

This idiom is used to describe making something more complicated than it needs to be. If someone says you are trying to **die bobbejaan agter die berg gaan haal** (pronounced: dee bob-uh-yahn ahkh-ter dee berg khahn haahl), it means you are trying to solve a problem in a difficult way when there might be an easier solution.

**Example:**

- **Jy probeer altyd die bobbejaan agter die berg gaan haal** – This means "You always try to make things more difficult than they need to be."

## "'n Appel val nie ver van die boom af nie"

**Literal meaning:** "An apple doesn't fall far from the tree."

This idiom is similar to the English saying, meaning that children often behave like their parents. If someone says **'n Appel val nie ver van die boom af nie** (pronounced: uh ahp-puhl fahl nee fehr fan dee bohm ahf nee), they are saying that a person is like their parents, whether in looks, personality, or behavior.

**Example:**

- **Hy is so slim soos sy pa, die appel val nie ver van die boom af nie** – This means "He is as smart as his father; the apple doesn't fall far from the tree."

## "Slaan twee vlieë met een klap"

**Literal meaning:** "Hit two flies with one slap."

This idiom is similar to the English phrase "kill two birds with one stone." It means accomplishing two things at the same time with one action. In Afrikaans, you can say **slaan twee vlieë met een klap** (pronounced: slahn tway flee-uh met een klahp) when you manage to do two things at once.

**Example:**

- **As ons vroeg vertrek, kan ons twee vlieë met een klap slaan** – This means "If we leave early, we can accomplish two things at once."

## "Die kat uit die sak laat"

**Literal meaning:** "Let the cat out of the bag."

Just like in English, this idiom means to reveal a secret. If someone accidentally or deliberately reveals a secret, you can say they **die kat uit die sak laat** (pronounced: dee kaht oyt dee sahk laat).

**Example:**

- **Sy het die kat uit die sak laat oor die partytjie** – This means "She let the secret out about the party."

## "Iemand oor die kole haal"

**Literal meaning:** "Pull someone over the coals."

This idiom means to criticize or scold someone harshly for making a mistake or doing something wrong. It's similar to the English phrase "rake someone over the coals." In Afrikaans, you can say **iemand oor die kole haal** (pronounced: ee-mant oor dee koh-luh haahl) when someone is being heavily criticized.

**Example:**

- **Die baas het my oor die kole gehaal oor die foute** – This means "The boss scolded me harshly for the mistakes."

## "Dis die einde van die wêreld"

**Literal meaning:** "It's the end of the world."

This idiom is used when something very serious or unfortunate happens, and it feels like everything is going wrong. In Afrikaans, **Dis die einde van die wêreld** (pronounced: dis dee ayn-duh fan dee veh-ruhld) means that things are really bad, but sometimes it's also used humorously for less serious situations.

**Example:**

- **Ek het my sleutel verloor, dis die einde van die wêreld** – This means "I lost my key; it's the end of the world."

## "Soos die hond in die bos"

**Literal meaning:** "Like the dog in the bush."

This idiom describes someone who feels lost or out of place in a situation. It's similar to the English expression "like a fish out of water." In Afrikaans, you can say **soos die hond in die bos** (pronounced: soos dee hont in dee bohss) when someone looks confused or doesn't know what to do.

**Example:**

- **Hy voel soos die hond in die bos by sy nuwe werk** – This means "He feels completely lost at his new job."

## "Om deur die blare te praat"

**Literal meaning:** "To talk through the leaves."

This idiom means to talk nonsense or say something that doesn't make sense. In Afrikaans, if someone is **deur die blare praat** (pronounced: deur dee blah-ruh praat), it means they're not being logical or their words are confusing.

**Example:**

- **Hy het deur die blare gepraat oor die toets** – This means "He talked nonsense about the test."

## Why Idioms Are Important

Idioms are an important part of any language because they give insight into the culture and thinking of the people who speak the language. In Afrikaans, idioms often reflect the daily life, animals, and environment of the people who use them. Learning idioms can help you sound more fluent and natural when speaking Afrikaans.

When using idioms, it's important to remember that they don't always translate directly into English, so you should focus on understanding the meaning rather than the literal words.

## Key Points to Remember

- **Idioms have special meanings**: An idiom is a phrase that doesn't always mean what the individual words say. It has a specific meaning that is understood by people who know the language.

- **Idioms reflect culture**: Many idioms in Afrikaans reflect the environment, animals, and everyday life of Afrikaans speakers, making them a unique part of the language.

- **Common idioms**: Some popular idioms include **die bobbejaan agter die berg gaan haal** (make things more complicated) and **die kat uit die sak laat** (reveal a secret).

- **Understanding idioms**: Learning idioms helps you sound more natural when speaking Afrikaans and allows you to understand more conversational expressions.

- **Idioms don't translate literally**: Don't try to translate idioms word for word. Focus on their meanings instead.

# Chapter 37

# Expressing Likes, Dislikes, and Preferences

In everyday conversations, people often talk about what they like and don't like. Whether you're talking about food, hobbies, or activities, knowing how to express your likes, dislikes, and preferences is very important. In Afrikaans, there are simple ways to say what you enjoy or prefer and what you don't. In this chapter, we will explore how to express your likes, dislikes, and preferences using common phrases, examples, and vocabulary.

## Talking About What You Like

The most basic way to say you like something in Afrikaans is by using the verb **hou van** (pronounced: hoh fan), which means "to like." This phrase is used to express liking something or someone. Let's start with a simple sentence structure for saying what you like:

- **Ek hou van...** – This means "I like..."

You can follow **Ek hou van...** with a noun or activity to describe what you enjoy. Here are some examples:

- **Ek hou van kos** (pronounced: ek hoh fan kohs) – This means "I like food."
- **Ek hou van musiek** (pronounced: ek hoh fan moo-seek) – This means "I like music."
- **Ek hou van lees** (pronounced: ek hoh fan lees) – This means "I like reading."
- **Ek hou van sokker** (pronounced: ek hoh fan soh-ker) – This means "I like soccer."

You can also use this phrase to talk about people or places you like:

- **Ek hou van my vriend** (pronounced: ek hoh fan may freend) – This means "I like my friend."

- **Ek hou van die strand** (pronounced: ek hoh fan dee strand) – This means "I like the beach."

## Talking About What You Don't Like

To talk about something you don't like in Afrikaans, you simply add the word **nie** (pronounced: nee) to make the sentence negative. The basic structure for expressing dislike is:

- **Ek hou nie van...** – This means "I don't like..."

Here are some examples of how to use this structure in sentences:

- **Ek hou nie van vis nie** (pronounced: ek hoh nee fan fis nee) – This means "I don't like fish."

- **Ek hou nie van dans nie** (pronounced: ek hoh nee fan dahns nee) – This means "I don't like dancing."

- **Ek hou nie van reën nie** (pronounced: ek hoh nee fan rayn nee) – This means "I don't like rain."

By adding **nie** twice in the sentence—once after the verb and again at the end—you can make it clear that you dislike something. This structure works with all kinds of activities, objects, or people.

## Expressing Preferences

When you want to say that you prefer one thing over another, you can use the verb **verkies** (pronounced: fer-kees), which means "to prefer." Here's how to express a preference in Afrikaans:

- **Ek verkies...** – This means "I prefer..."

For example:

- **Ek verkies koffie** (pronounced: ek fer-kees kof-fee) – This means "I prefer coffee."

- **Ek verkies koeldrank** (pronounced: ek fer-kees kool-drahngk) – This means "I prefer soda."

- **Ek verkies honde bo katte** (pronounced: ek fer-kees hon-de boh kaht-te) – This means "I prefer dogs over cats."

When expressing preferences between two things, you can use the word **bo** (pronounced: boh), which means "over" or "instead of." You can also add more details to your preferences by explaining why you prefer one thing over another.

## Asking About Likes and Dislikes

If you want to ask someone what they like or don't like, you can use a few simple question structures. Here are some examples:

- **Hou jy van...?** (pronounced: hoh yay fan...?) – This means "Do you like...?"

- **Verkies jy...?** (pronounced: fer-kees yay...?) – This means "Do you prefer...?"

Let's look at how you can use these in sentences:

- **Hou jy van sokker?** (pronounced: hoh yay fan soh-ker) – This means "Do you like soccer?"

- **Verkies jy melk of water?** (pronounced: fer-kees yay melk awf vah-ter) – This means "Do you prefer milk or water?"

These questions are useful when you want to ask someone about their likes and preferences, whether it's for food, sports, or other activities.

## Adding More Detail to Your Preferences

Once you know how to express your likes and dislikes, you can add more detail to explain why you like or dislike something. Here are some phrases you can use to give reasons:

- **Omdat...** (pronounced: om-daht) – This means "because."

- **Ek hou van sokker omdat dit lekker is** (pronounced: ek hoh fan soh-ker om-daht dit lek-ker is) – This means "I like soccer because it's fun."

- **Ek verkies koffie omdat dit my wakker maak** (pronounced: ek fer-kees kof-fee om-daht dit may vak-ker mahk) – This means "I prefer coffee because it wakes me up."

Adding **omdat** to your sentence allows you to explain the reasons behind your preferences. This makes your conversation more interesting and gives others a better understanding of your likes and dislikes.

## Expressing Strong Likes or Dislikes

Sometimes, you may want to express that you really like or really dislike something. To do this, you can add the word **baie** (pronounced: bah-yuh), which means "very" or "a lot," to your sentences. Here's how you can use it:

- **Ek hou baie van...** – This means "I really like..."

- **Ek hou baie van kos** (pronounced: ek hoh bah-yuh fan kohs) – This means "I really like food."

- **Ek hou baie van lees** (pronounced: ek hoh bah-yuh fan lees) – This means "I really like reading."

If you want to express that you really dislike something, you can use the structure **Ek hou glad nie van...** (pronounced: ek hoh glad nee fan...), which means "I don't like... at all." Here are some examples:

- **Ek hou glad nie van vis nie** (pronounced: ek hoh glad nee fan fis nee) – This means "I don't like fish at all."

- **Ek hou glad nie van sokker nie** (pronounced: ek hoh glad nee fan soh-ker nee) – This means "I don't like soccer at all."

Using **baie** and **glad nie** helps you express strong feelings about your preferences, making it clear whether you really like or strongly dislike something.

## Talking About Favorite Things

In addition to talking about likes and dislikes, you may want to express what your favorite things are. To say "favorite" in Afrikaans, you use the word **gunsteling** (pronounced: khun-steh-ling). Here's how you can talk about your favorite things:

- **My gunsteling kos is pizza** (pronounced: may khun-steh-ling kohs is pit-zah) – This means "My favorite food is pizza."

- **My gunsteling kleur is blou** (pronounced: may khun-steh-ling kleer is bloh) – This means "My favorite color is blue."

You can use the word **gunsteling** before any noun to describe your favorite food, color, sport, or anything else.

## Key Points to Remember

- **Expressing likes**: Use **Ek hou van...** (I like...) to talk about things you enjoy.

- **Expressing dislikes**: Use **Ek hou nie van...** (I don't like...) to talk about things you dislike.

- **Expressing preferences**: Use **Ek verkies...** (I prefer...) to say what you prefer.

- **Asking about likes and dislikes**: Use **Hou jy van...?** (Do you like...?) or **Verkies jy...?** (Do you prefer...?) to ask someone about their preferences.

- **Expressing strong likes or dislikes**: Use **Ek hou baie van...** (I really like...) or **Ek hou glad nie van...** (I don't like... at all) to express strong feelings about your likes and dislikes.

# Chapter 38

# Talking About Hobbies and Interests

Everyone has hobbies and interests that they enjoy in their free time. Some people love playing sports, while others enjoy reading or drawing. In this chapter, you will learn how to talk about your hobbies and interests in Afrikaans. You'll also learn how to ask others about their hobbies, as well as how to describe activities you like to do. Let's explore some common vocabulary, phrases, and examples to help you express your hobbies and interests confidently in Afrikaans.

## Common Vocabulary for Hobbies and Interests

First, let's start with some words that describe common hobbies and interests. These are activities that people often do for fun or relaxation:

- **Lees** (pronounced: lees) – This means "reading."

- **Skilder** (pronounced: skil-der) – This means "painting."

- **Teken** (pronounced: tee-ken) – This means "drawing."

- **Sport** (pronounced: sport) – This means "sports."

- **Dans** (pronounced: dahns) – This means "dancing."

- **Musiek** (pronounced: moo-seek) – This means "music."

- **Fotografie** (pronounced: foh-toh-ghrah-fee) – This means "photography."

- **Kook** (pronounced: kook) – This means "cooking."

- **Speel videospeletjies** (pronounced: speel vee-dee-oh-spee-lay-kheys) – This means "playing video games."

- **Fietsry** (pronounced: feets-ray) – This means "cycling" or "riding a bicycle."

These words will help you talk about the activities you like to do. Now, let's see how you can use them in sentences.

## Talking About Your Hobbies

The easiest way to talk about your hobbies in Afrikaans is to use the phrase **Ek hou van...**, which means "I like..." You can then add the hobby or activity you enjoy. Here are some examples:

- **Ek hou van lees** (pronounced: ek hoh fan lees) – This means "I like reading."
- **Ek hou van musiek** (pronounced: ek hoh fan moo-seek) – This means "I like music."
- **Ek hou van teken** (pronounced: ek hoh fan tee-ken) – This means "I like drawing."
- **Ek hou van sport** (pronounced: ek hoh fan sport) – This means "I like sports."

You can also talk about your hobbies by describing what you do with the phrase **Ek speel...** (pronounced: ek speel), which means "I play." For example:

- **Ek speel sokker** (pronounced: ek speel soh-ker) – This means "I play soccer."
- **Ek speel kitaar** (pronounced: ek speel kee-tar) – This means "I play guitar."

## Describing How Often You Do Your Hobbies

Once you know how to say what hobbies you enjoy, you can describe how often you do them. Here are some useful phrases for talking about how frequently you engage in your hobbies:

- **Elke dag** (pronounced: el-kuh dahkh) – This means "every day."
- **Een keer per week** (pronounced: een keer per vake) – This means "once a week."
- **Baie dikwels** (pronounced: bah-yuh dik-fels) – This means "very often."
- **Soms** (pronounced: sohms) – This means "sometimes."
- **Selde** (pronounced: sel-duh) – This means "rarely."

Here are some examples of how to use these phrases:

- **Ek lees elke dag** (pronounced: ek lees el-kuh dahkh) – This means "I read every day."

- **Ek teken een keer per week** (pronounced: ek tee-ken een keer per vake) – This means "I draw once a week."

- **Ek speel sokker soms** (pronounced: ek speel soh-ker sohms) – This means "I play soccer sometimes."

Using these phrases helps add more detail to your sentences when talking about your hobbies and interests.

## Asking Others About Their Hobbies

If you want to ask someone about their hobbies and interests, you can use the question **Wat is jou stokperdjies?** (pronounced: vaht is yow stok-perd-jees), which means "What are your hobbies?" You can also ask specific questions like:

- **Hou jy van lees?** (pronounced: hoh yay fan lees) – This means "Do you like reading?"

- **Speel jy sokker?** (pronounced: speel yay soh-ker) – This means "Do you play soccer?"

- **Wat doen jy in jou vrye tyd?** (pronounced: vaht doon yay in yow fray-uh tayt) – This means "What do you do in your free time?"

These questions are a great way to learn more about someone else's hobbies and start a conversation about shared interests.

## Talking About Interests

In addition to hobbies, you might want to talk about your general interests—things you enjoy learning about or talking about. In Afrikaans, you can use the phrase **Ek stel belang in...** (pronounced: ek stel buh-lung in...), which means "I am interested in..."

Here are some examples of how to use this phrase:

- **Ek stel belang in wetenskap** (pronounced: ek stel buh-lung in veht-en-skhahp) – This means "I am interested in science."

- **Ek stel belang in geskiedenis** (pronounced: ek stel buh-lung in ghuh-skee-den-iss) – This means "I am interested in history."

- **Ek stel belang in sport** (pronounced: ek stel buh-lung in sport) – This means "I am interested in sports."

You can use this structure to talk about any subject or topic you're interested in, whether it's science, history, or something else.

## Describing Hobbies You Don't Enjoy

Just as important as talking about what you like is being able to say what you don't like. You can do this by using the phrase **Ek hou nie van...** (pronounced: ek hoh nee fan...), which means "I don't like..." Here are some examples:

- **Ek hou nie van dans nie** (pronounced: ek hoh nee fan dahns nee) – This means "I don't like dancing."

- **Ek hou nie van skilder nie** (pronounced: ek hoh nee fan skil-der nee) – This means "I don't like painting."

You can use this phrase to describe any hobby or activity that you don't enjoy.

## Talking About Future Hobbies

You might want to talk about hobbies or activities you'd like to try in the future. In Afrikaans, you can use the phrase **Ek wil graag...** (pronounced: ek vil ghrahkh...), which means "I would like to..." Here's how to use it in sentences:

- **Ek wil graag leer om kitaar te speel** (pronounced: ek vil ghrahkh leer om kee-tar tuh speel) – This means "I would like to learn to play guitar."

- **Ek wil graag dansklasse neem** (pronounced: ek vil ghrahkh dahns-klah-suh neem) – This means "I would like to take dance classes."

Using this structure, you can talk about hobbies you want to explore in the future.

## Key Points to Remember

- **Talking about hobbies**: Use the phrase **Ek hou van...** (I like...) to talk about activities you enjoy, like reading or playing sports.

- **Asking about hobbies**: Use **Wat is jou stokperdjies?** (What are your hobbies?) or **Wat doen jy in jou vrye tyd?** (What do you do in your free time?) to ask others about their hobbies.

- **Describing interests**: Use **Ek stel belang in...** (I am interested in...) to talk about subjects or topics you enjoy learning about.

- **Talking about future hobbies**: Use **Ek wil graag...** (I would like to...) to describe hobbies or activities you want to try in the future.

- **Describing frequency**: Use phrases like **Elke dag** (Every day) or **Soms** (Sometimes) to describe how often you do your hobbies.

# Chapter 39

# Writing in Afrikaans: Simple Sentences

Learning how to write simple sentences is an important step when starting to learn Afrikaans. Writing allows you to practice forming sentences and helps you understand how the language works. In this chapter, we will start with the basics of sentence structure in Afrikaans and build on that to create simple sentences. We'll cover subjects, verbs, and objects, as well as how to add details like adjectives and adverbs.

## Basic Sentence Structure

In Afrikaans, the basic sentence structure is similar to English. A simple sentence usually follows the Subject-Verb-Object (SVO) pattern. This means that the subject (who or what is doing the action) comes first, followed by the verb (the action), and then the object (who or what the action is happening to). Let's look at some examples:

- **Ek lees 'n boek** (pronounced: ek lees uh book) – This means "I am reading a book."

- **Hy eet 'n appel** (pronounced: hay eet uh ah-puhl) – This means "He is eating an apple."

- **Sy speel sokker** (pronounced: say speel soh-ker) – This means "She is playing soccer."

In these sentences, **Ek**, **Hy**, and **Sy** are the subjects, **lees**, **eet**, and **speel** are the verbs, and **'n boek**, **'n appel**, and **sokker** are the objects. This is the basic structure of most simple sentences in Afrikaans.

## Using Verbs in Simple Sentences

Verbs are important in every sentence because they describe the action. In Afrikaans, verbs usually come after the subject, as shown in the examples above. Let's look at more verbs you can use in your sentences:

- **Lees** (pronounced: lees) – This means "read."

- **Eet** (pronounced: eet) – This means "eat."

- **Skryf** (pronounced: skrayf) – This means "write."

- **Loop** (pronounced: lohp) – This means "walk."

- **Speel** (pronounced: speel) – This means "play."

- **Swem** (pronounced: swehm) – This means "swim."

Here are some more examples using different verbs:

- **Ek skryf 'n brief** (pronounced: ek skrayf uh breef) – This means "I am writing a letter."

- **Hulle loop na die park** (pronounced: huh-luh lohp nah dee park) – This means "They are walking to the park."

- **Ons swem in die see** (pronounced: ohns swehm in dee say) – This means "We are swimming in the sea."

When writing in Afrikaans, make sure to place the verb right after the subject to create a simple and clear sentence.

## Using Pronouns as Subjects

In Afrikaans, just like in English, we often use pronouns (words like "I," "you," "he," and "they") as subjects in sentences. Here are the most common pronouns in Afrikaans:

- **Ek** (pronounced: ek) – This means "I."

- **Jy** (pronounced: yay) – This means "you."

- **Hy** (pronounced: hay) – This means "he."

- **Sy** (pronounced: say) – This means "she."

- **Ons** (pronounced: ohns) – This means "we."

- **Hulle** (pronounced: huh-luh) – This means "they."

Here are some examples of how to use these pronouns in sentences:

- **Ek eet 'n toebroodjie** (pronounced: ek eet uh too-broo-jee) – This means "I am eating a sandwich."

- **Jy lees die koerant** (pronounced: yay lees dee koo-rant) – This means "You are reading the newspaper."

- **Hulle speel in die tuin** (pronounced: huh-luh speel in dee tayn) – This means "They are playing in the garden."

Using pronouns makes sentences easier and faster to write. In most simple sentences, the pronoun will come first, followed by the verb and then the object.

## Adding Adjectives to Sentences

Adjectives are words that describe nouns, such as "big," "small," "happy," or "fun." In Afrikaans, adjectives usually come before the noun they describe, just like in English. Here are some common adjectives:

- **Groot** (pronounced: khroot) – This means "big."

- **Klein** (pronounced: klayn) – This means "small."

- **Mooi** (pronounced: moy) – This means "beautiful."

- **Interessant** (pronounced: in-te-re-sant) – This means "interesting."

- **Lekker** (pronounced: lek-ker) – This means "nice" or "fun."

Let's add these adjectives to some sentences:

- **Ek lees 'n interessante boek** (pronounced: ek lees uh in-te-re-sant-uh book) – This means "I am reading an interesting book."

- **Sy eet 'n groot appel** (pronounced: say eet uh khroot ah-puhl) – This means "She is eating a big apple."

- **Ons speel in die lekker tuin** (pronounced: ohns speel in dee lek-ker tayn) – This means "We are playing in the nice garden."

Adjectives help to give more details to your sentences, making them more descriptive and interesting.

## Using Adverbs to Describe Actions

Adverbs describe how, when, or where something happens. They usually go after the verb in a sentence. Here are some common adverbs in Afrikaans:

- **Vinnig** (pronounced: fin-nikh) – This means "quickly."

- **Stadig** (pronounced: stah-dikh) – This means "slowly."

- **Nou** (pronounced: noh) – This means "now."

- **Vandag** (pronounced: fan-dahkh) – This means "today."

- **Oral** (pronounced: oh-ral) – This means "everywhere."

Here are some examples of how to use adverbs in sentences:

- **Ek lees vinnig** (pronounced: ek lees fin-nikh) – This means "I read quickly."

- **Hulle eet stadig** (pronounced: huh-luh eet stah-dikh) – This means "They eat slowly."

- **Sy speel nou** (pronounced: say speel noh) – This means "She is playing now."

Using adverbs helps explain how or when an action takes place, adding more meaning to your sentences.

## Forming Questions in Simple Sentences

When asking questions in Afrikaans, you often switch the subject and the verb. For example, in English, you might say "Are you eating?" In Afrikaans, you would say **Eet jy?** (pronounced: eet yay), which is the same structure as "Eating you?" Here are some examples of how to form questions:

- **Lees jy die boek?** (pronounced: lees yay dee book) – This means "Are you reading the book?"

- **Eet hulle appels?** (pron ounced: eet huh-luh ah-puls) – This means "Are they eating apples?"

- **Speel jy sokker?** (pronounced: speel yay soh-ker) – This means "Are you playing soccer?"

Switching the verb and subject allows you to turn a simple statement into a question. This is a useful way to start conversations and ask about different actions in Afrikaans.

## Key Points to Remember

- **Basic sentence structure**: In Afrikaans, the basic sentence structure is Subject-Verb-Object, just like in English.

- **Using verbs**: Verbs describe actions in sentences. Common verbs include **lees** (read), **eet** (eat), and **speel** (play).

- **Using adjectives**: Adjectives describe nouns and come before the noun. Words like **groot** (big) and **mooi** (beautiful) help make sentences more descriptive.

- **Using adverbs**: Adverbs describe how or when an action happens. Common adverbs include **vinnig** (quickly) and **stadig** (slowly).

- **Forming questions**: To ask questions, switch the subject and verb, like **Lees jy?** (Are you reading?).

# Chapter 40

# Politeness and Etiquette in Afrikaans

Politeness is an important part of communication in any language, and Afrikaans is no different. Being polite shows respect and consideration for others, and knowing how to express politeness can help you make a good impression. In this chapter, we will explore some key phrases and etiquette rules that will help you communicate politely in Afrikaans. We'll cover greetings, thanking, apologizing, and asking for things in a polite way.

## Greetings: Starting Polite Conversations

Greeting people politely is the first step in any conversation. In Afrikaans, there are a few common ways to greet others, depending on the time of day and the formality of the situation. Here are some polite greetings you can use:

- **Goeie môre** (pronounced: ghoy-uh mor-ruh) – This means "Good morning."

- **Goeie middag** (pronounced: ghoy-uh mid-dahkh) – This means "Good afternoon."

- **Goeie naand** (pronounced: ghoy-uh nahnt) – This means "Good evening."

- **Hallo** (pronounced: hah-loh) – This means "Hello." It's a more casual greeting.

When greeting someone politely, it's always a good idea to follow up with **Hoe gaan dit met jou?** (pronounced: hoo khahn dit met yow), which means "How are you?" This shows that you're interested in the person's well-being.

## Thanking Someone: Showing Appreciation

Saying "thank you" is a key part of being polite. In Afrikaans, there are several ways to express gratitude, depending on how formal the situation is. Here are some common ways to thank someone:

- **Dankie** (pronounced: dun-kee) – This means "Thank you."

- **Baie dankie** (pronounced: bah-yuh dun-kee) – This means "Thank you very much."

- **Dankie, ek waardeer dit** (pronounced: dun-kee ek vahr-deer dit) – This means "Thank you, I appreciate it."

If you want to respond to someone thanking you, you can say **Dis 'n plesier** (pronounced: dis uh pleh-seer), which means "It's a pleasure." This is a polite way to say "You're welcome."

## Apologizing: Saying Sorry

Sometimes, you may need to apologize if you've made a mistake or caused inconvenience. Here are some polite ways to say "sorry" in Afrikaans:

- **Ek is jammer** (pronounced: ek is yah-mer) – This means "I am sorry."

- **Verskoon my** (pronounced: fer-skohn may) – This means "Excuse me" or "Pardon me."

- **Ek vra om verskoning** (pronounced: ek frah om fer-skoe-ning) – This means "I apologize."

If someone apologizes to you, a polite response is **Dis reg** (pronounced: dis rekh), which means "It's okay" or "That's fine."

## Asking Politely: Using "Please"

When asking for something, using the word "please" is a simple way to show politeness. In Afrikaans, the word for "please" is **asseblief** (pronounced: ah-suh-bleef). Here are some examples of how to use it:

- **Kan jy asseblief vir my help?** (pronounced: kahn yay ah-suh-bleef fer may help) – This means "Can you please help me?"

- **Mag ek asseblief 'n glas water hê?** (pronounced: mahkh ek ah-suh-bleef uh glahs vah-ter heh) – This means "May I please have a glass of water?"

- **Gee asseblief die boek** (pronounced: gheh ah-suh-bleef dee book) – This means "Please give me the book."

Adding **asseblief** to your sentences makes your request polite and respectful.

## Responding Politely to Questions

When someone asks you a question, it's important to respond politely, even if you don't know the answer or can't help. Here are some polite responses:

- **Ja, asseblief** (pronounced: yah ah-suh-bleef) – This means "Yes, please."

- **Nee, dankie** (pronounced: nee dun-kee) – This means "No, thank you."

- **Ek weet nie** (pronounced: ek veet nee) – This means "I don't know."

- **Ek sal dit probeer** (pronounced: ek sahl dit proh-beer) – This means "I will try."

Even when you don't have the answer or can't fulfill a request, responding politely shows respect for the person asking.

## Being Polite in Social Settings

In social situations, being polite goes beyond just saying "please" and "thank you." It's also about being respectful of others' feelings and space. Here are some general etiquette tips for social settings in Afrikaans-speaking cultures:

- When greeting someone, it's polite to make eye contact and shake hands. In formal settings, a slight bow or nod of the head is also appropriate.

- If you're entering someone's home, it's polite to say **Dankie dat ek hier kan wees** (pronounced: dun-kee daht ek heer kahn vays), which means "Thank you for having me."

- If you want to offer someone something, like food or a seat, you can say **Kan ek asseblief vir jou aanbied?** (pronounced: kahn ek ah-suh-bleef fer yow ahn-beet), which means "Can I offer you something?"

- When leaving a gathering, it's polite to say **Tot siens** (pronounced: toht seens), which means "Goodbye," or **Baie dankie vir alles** (pronounced: bah-yuh dun-kee fer ah-les), which means "Thank you very much for everything."

## Formal and Informal Politeness

In Afrikaans, just like in English, there are different levels of formality. The way you speak to your friends may be more casual than the way you speak to an adult, teacher, or someone in authority. Here are some ways to adjust your politeness depending on the situation:

- For formal situations, use **u** (pronounced: oo) instead of **jy** (you). For example, **Kan u asseblief kom?** (pronounced: kahn oo ah-suh-bleef kom), which means "Can you please come?"

- In informal situations, it's okay to be more relaxed with language. For example, you might say **Kan jy my help?** (pronounced: kahn yay may help), which means "Can you help me?"

Always be mindful of who you're speaking to and adjust your level of politeness to suit the situation.

## Expressing Gratitude in Afrikaans

Expressing gratitude is not just about saying "thank you." It's also about showing appreciation for someone's help or kindness. Here are some additional ways to express gratitude in Afrikaans:

- **Ek waardeer dit baie** (pronounced: ek vahr-deer dit bah-yuh) – This means "I appreciate it a lot."

- **Dit is baie gaaf van jou** (pronounced: dit is bah-yuh khahf fan yow) – This means "That's very kind of you."

- **Dankie dat jy my gehelp het** (pronounced: dun-kee daht yay may ghuh-help het) – This means "Thank you for helping me."

Gratitude is a key part of politeness, and expressing it shows that you recognize and value the other person's efforts.

## Key Points to Remember

- **Polite greetings**: Use phrases like **Goeie môre** (Good morning) and **Hoe gaan dit met jou?** (How are you?) to greet people politely.

- **Thanking and apologizing**: Use **Dankie** (Thank you) and **Ek is jammer** (I am sorry) to show politeness in different situations.

- **Using "please"**: Always use **asseblief** when asking for something to make your request polite.

- **Formal and informal politeness**: Use **u** (you) in formal situations and **jy** in informal ones, adjusting your politeness to suit the context.

- **Responding politely**: Use polite responses like **Ja, asseblief** (Yes, please) and **Nee, dankie** (No, thank you) in conversations.

# Chapter 41

# Talking About Hopes, Plans, and Dreams

Everyone has hopes, dreams, and plans for the future. Whether you dream of becoming a doctor, plan to travel the world, or hope to achieve something special, it's important to know how to talk about these things in Afrikaans. In this chapter, we will learn how to express your hopes, plans, and dreams in simple Afrikaans sentences. You will also learn how to ask others about their hopes and plans and how to use key phrases to describe what you want to achieve in life.

## Expressing Hopes

When we talk about hope, we're usually thinking about something good that we want to happen in the future. In Afrikaans, the word for "hope" is **hoop** (pronounced: hohp). Here are some ways you can use it in sentences:

- **Ek hoop...** – This means "I hope..."

- **Ek hoop ek kan dit doen** (pronounced: ek hohp ek kahn dit doon) – This means "I hope I can do it."

- **Ek hoop dit gaan goed** (pronounced: ek hohp dit khahn khood) – This means "I hope it goes well."

When expressing hope, you can use **Ek hoop** followed by something you want to happen. For example:

- **Ek hoop ons wen die wedstryd** (pronounced: ek hohp ohns ven dee veht-strayd) – This means "I hope we win the game."

- **Ek hoop ek slaag die toets** (pronounced: ek hohp ek slahkh dee toost) – This means "I hope I pass the test."

## Expressing Dreams

Dreams are often things we imagine for our future, like what we want to become or where we want to go. The word for "dream" in Afrikaans is **droom** (pronounced: drehm). Here are some ways to talk about your dreams:

- **Ek droom daarvan om...** – This means "I dream of..."

Here are some examples:

- **Ek droom daarvan om 'n dokter te wees** (pronounced: ek drehm dah-vahn om uh dok-ter tuh vees) – This means "I dream of being a doctor."

- **Ek droom daarvan om die wêreld te reis** (pronounced: ek drehm dah-vahn om dee veh-rold tuh rays) – This means "I dream of traveling the world."

- **Ek droom daarvan om musiek te maak** (pronounced: ek drehm dah-vahn om moo-seek tuh mahk) – This means "I dream of making music."

Talking about dreams is a way to express what you imagine for your future, whether it's a career, traveling, or achieving something special.

## Talking About Your Plans

Plans are things you want to do in the near or distant future. The word for "plan" in Afrikaans is **plan** (pronounced: plahn). To talk about your plans, you can use the phrase **Ek beplan om...** (pronounced: ek buh-plahn om...), which means "I plan to...". Here are some examples:

- **Ek beplan om hard te werk** (pronounced: ek buh-plahn om hart tuh verk) – This means "I plan to work hard."

- **Ek beplan om te studeer** (pronounced: ek buh-plahn om tuh stoo-deer) – This means "I plan to study."

- **Ek beplan om 'n huis te koop** (pronounced: ek buh-plahn om uh hays tuh kohp) – This means "I plan to buy a house."

Talking about your plans shows others what you are preparing for in the future, whether it's working, studying, or making big decisions.

## Asking Others About Their Hopes and Dreams

If you want to ask someone about their hopes, plans, or dreams, there are simple questions you can use. Here are some helpful questions to start a conversation:

- **Wat hoop jy?** (pronounced: vaht hohp yay) – This means "What do you hope for?"

- **Wat is jou droom?** (pronounced: vaht is yow drehm) – This means "What is your dream?"

- **Wat beplan jy vir die toekoms?** (pronounced: vaht buh-plahn yay fer dee too-koms) – This means "What are you planning for the future?"

Asking someone about their hopes, dreams, and plans can help you learn more about them and their goals.

## Talking About Your Future Goals

When talking about what you want to achieve in the future, the word **doel** (pronounced: dool) means "goal." You can use the phrase **My doel is om...** (pronounced: may dool is om...), which means "My goal is to...". Here are some examples:

- **My doel is om 'n suksesvolle persoon te wees** (pronounced: may dool is om uh suhk-ses-fohl-uh per-soon tuh vees) – This means "My goal is to be a successful person."

- **My doel is om 'n kampioen te word** (pronounced: may dool is om uh kahm-pee-oon tuh vort) – This means "My goal is to become a champion."

- **My doel is om goed te doen in die skool** (pronounced: may dool is om khoot tuh doon in dee skohl) – This means "My goal is to do well in school."

Setting goals for the future helps you focus on what you want to achieve and gives you something to work toward.

## Using "Would Like" for Hopes and Plans

When talking about things you hope or plan to do, you might also want to say "would like." In Afrikaans, you can use the phrase **Ek sal graag...** (pronounced: ek sahl ghrahkh), which means "I would like to...". Here are some examples:

- **Ek sal graag 'n nuwe vaardigheid leer** (pronounced: ek sahl ghrahkh uh nee-vuh fahr-di-kayt leer) – This means "I would like to learn a new skill."

- **Ek sal graag in 'n ander land werk** (pronounced: ek sahl ghrahkh in uh ahn-der lahnt verk) – This means "I would like to work in another country."

- **Ek sal graag meer vriende hê** (pronounced: ek sahl ghrahkh meer free-nde heh) – This means "I would like to have more friends."

Using "would like" in your sentences is a polite way to express your hopes or desires for the future.

## Talking About Long-Term and Short-Term Plans

Sometimes, you might want to talk about things you plan to do soon, and other times you may talk about long-term goals. In Afrikaans, you can use these phrases:

- **Korttermyn** (pronounced: kort-ter-main) – This means "short-term."

- **Langtermyn** (pronounced: lahng-ter-main) – This means "long-term."

Here are some examples:

- **My korttermyn plan is om meer te oefen** (pronounced: may kort-ter-main plahn is om meer tuh oo-fen) – This means "My short-term plan is to exercise more."

- **My langtermyn doel is om 'n huis te bou** (pronounced: may lahng-ter-main dool is om uh hays tuh boh) – This means "My long-term goal is to build a house."

Knowing how to talk about both short-term and long-term goals helps you express a variety of plans for the future.

## Using "Hopefully" in Afrikaans

Sometimes, when we talk about hopes or dreams, we use the word "hopefully." In Afrikaans, you can say **hopelik** (pronounced: hoh-peh-lik). Here's how to use it in sentences:

- **Hopelik sal ons môre wen** (pronounced: hoh-peh-lik sahl ohns moh-ruh ven) – This means "Hopefully, we will win tomorrow."

- **Hopelik kan ek volgende jaar reis** (pronounced: hoh-peh-lik kahn ek foh-khen-deh yah-r rays) – This means "Hopefully, I can travel next year."

Using "hopefully" allows you to express that you are optimistic about something happening in the future.

## Key Points to Remember

- **Expressing hope**: Use **Ek hoop...** (I hope...) to talk about something you wish for in the future.

- **Expressing dreams**: Use **Ek droom daarvan om...** (I dream of...) to describe what you imagine for the future.

- **Talking about plans**: Use **Ek beplan om...** (I plan to...) to describe what you are preparing to do.

- **Talking about goals**: Use **My doel is om...** (My goal is to...) to express your future achievements.

- **Asking about hopes and dreams**: Use questions like **Wat hoop jy?** (What do you hope for?) to ask others about their hopes and plans.

# Chapter 42

# Cultural References and Traditions

When learning a language, it's important to understand the culture that comes with it. In this chapter, we will explore some of the cultural references and traditions that are common in Afrikaans-speaking communities, especially in South Africa. These traditions reflect the history, values, and lifestyle of the people who speak Afrikaans. We will learn about holidays, celebrations, foods, and customs that are part of the Afrikaans culture. By understanding these cultural elements, you can better connect with the language and the people who speak it.

## Public Holidays and Celebrations

Like many countries, South Africa has public holidays that reflect its history and culture. Some of these holidays are especially important to Afrikaans-speaking communities. Here are a few key holidays:

- **Nuwejaar** (pronounced: noo-vuh-yahr) – This means "New Year's Day." On January 1st, families and friends gather to celebrate the start of the new year. It's a time for parties, fireworks, and good food.

- **Geloftedag** (pronounced: ghuh-lof-tuh-dahkh) – This means "Day of the Vow." Celebrated on December 16th, it commemorates a significant event in Afrikaner history when the Voortrekkers made a vow before the Battle of Blood River in 1838. It's a day for remembering the faith and courage of early Afrikaners.

- **Kersfees** (pronounced: kers-fees) – This means "Christmas." Afrikaans-speaking families celebrate Christmas on December 25th with a mix of traditional Christian customs, including church services, family gatherings, and festive meals.

These holidays are important times for family and community gatherings, and they give us a window into the values and beliefs of Afrikaans-speaking people.

## Family Traditions

Family is very important in Afrikaans culture. Family gatherings often take place around holidays, but they can also happen on weekends or during important events like birthdays and anniversaries. One common tradition is the **braai** (pronounced: bry), which is a barbecue. A braai is more than just cooking food over a fire; it's a time for socializing and spending quality time with loved ones.

- **Ons gaan braai** (pronounced: ohns ghahn bry) – This means "We are going to have a barbecue."

- **Vleis** (pronounced: flays) – This means "meat," which is a key part of a braai. Popular meats include steak, sausage, and lamb chops.

Braais often include salads, breads, and desserts. The relaxed and friendly atmosphere of a braai makes it a favorite way for Afrikaans families and friends to spend time together.

## Traditional Foods

Food is an important part of any culture, and Afrikaans-speaking people have some delicious traditional dishes. Here are a few you might encounter:

- **Bobotie** (pronounced: buh-boh-tee) – This is a savory dish made with spiced minced meat, topped with an egg mixture, and baked. It is often served with yellow rice.

- **Melktert** (pronounced: melk-tert) – This is a sweet custard tart made with milk, sugar, and a pastry crust. It's a popular dessert in Afrikaans homes.

- **Boerewors** (pronounced: boo-ruh-vors) – This is a type of sausage that is typically grilled at a braai. The name means "farmer's sausage."

- **Biltong** (pronounced: bil-tong) – This is dried, cured meat that is similar to beef jerky. It's a popular snack.

These foods are not just delicious; they are also connected to the history and farming lifestyle of many Afrikaans-speaking people. Many of these dishes have been passed down through generations and are enjoyed during special occasions and family meals.

## Language and Proverbs

Afrikaans is a language rich in idiomatic expressions and proverbs that reflect the values and wisdom of its speakers. Here are a few common Afrikaans proverbs and sayings:

- **Stille waters, diepe grond** (pronounced: sti-luh vah-ters dee-puh grohnd) – This means "Still waters run deep." It's used to describe someone who may appear quiet or reserved but has deep thoughts or strong feelings.

- **Elke hond kry sy dag** (pronounced: el-kuh hond krey say dahkh) – This means "Every dog has his day." It's a way of saying that everyone will have their moment of success or good fortune.

- **Wie nie waag nie, wen nie** (pronounced: vee nee vahkh nee ven nee) – This means "Nothing ventured, nothing gained." It encourages people to take risks if they want to achieve something.

These proverbs offer a glimpse into the values of the Afrikaans-speaking community, such as the importance of perseverance, caution, and taking opportunities when they arise.

## Religious Practices

Many Afrikaans-speaking people follow the Christian faith, and religion plays an important role in their daily lives and traditions. Sundays are often reserved for attending church services, and many families come together for Sunday lunch afterward. Holidays like **Kersfees** (Christmas) and **Paasfees** (pronounced: pahs-fees), meaning "Easter," are celebrated with special meals and church services.

A common saying in Afrikaans is **God seën jou** (pronounced: ghot sayn yow), which means "God bless you." This is often said to express goodwill and kindness to others.

## Sports and Recreation

Sports are an important part of life for many Afrikaans-speaking people, especially rugby. Rugby is often described as a national sport in South Africa, and many Afrikaans families enjoy watching and playing it. Some popular teams are the **Springbokke** (pronounced: spring-bok-uh), which is the South African national rugby team.

Another popular sport is **krieket** (pronounced: kree-ket), which means "cricket." Cricket matches are often watched with family and friends, and it's common for people to spend time outdoors playing sports or enjoying nature.

When talking about sports, you can use these phrases:

- **Ek speel rugby** (pronounced: ek speel rahg-bee) – This means "I play rugby."

- **Ons kyk krieket** (pronounced: ohns kayk kree-ket) – This means "We are watching cricket."

## Music and Dance

Music is an important part of Afrikaans culture, with many traditional songs passed down through generations. **Boeremusiek** (pronounced: boo-ruh-moo-seek), or "farmers' music," is a style of folk music that originated with the Afrikaner farming communities. It often includes instruments like the accordion and violin.

Dancing is also a popular part of social events, especially at festivals and weddings. The **langarm** (pronounced: lahng-ahrm) is a traditional Afrikaans dance style, where couples dance together with their arms extended, moving in smooth, flowing movements.

## Festivals and Community Events

There are many festivals in South Africa that celebrate Afrikaans culture, music, and traditions. One of the biggest is the **Klein Karoo Nasionale Kunstefees** (pronounced: klayn kah-roo nah-see-oh-nah-luh kuns-teh-fees), which is a national arts festival held in the town of Oudtshoorn. It's a week-long celebration of Afrikaans arts, including music, theater, and visual arts.

Community events like **boeremarkte** (pronounced: boo-ruh-mark-teh), or farmers' markets, are also popular. Here, people gather to buy and sell homemade goods, fresh produce, and crafts, all while enjoying the company of their neighbors.

## Key Points to Remember

- **Holidays and celebrations**: Afrikaans-speaking communities celebrate holidays like **Kersfees** (Christmas), **Nuwejaar** (New Year's), and **Geloftedag** (Day of the Vow).

- **Family traditions**: The **braai** is an important family gathering where people cook and eat together.

- **Traditional foods** : Dishes like **bobotie**, **melktert**, and **biltong** are popular in Afrikaans culture.

- **Sports and music**: Rugby and cricket are beloved sports, and **boeremusiek** is a traditional style of music.

- **Festivals and events**: Festivals like the **Klein Karoo Nasionale Kunstefees** celebrate Afrikaans arts and culture.

# Chapter 43

# Formal and Informal Afrikaans: Register and Tone

When learning a new language like Afrikaans, it's important to know how to use the language in different situations. This means understanding when to use formal or informal language. In Afrikaans, just like in English, how you speak to your friends may be different from how you speak to your teacher or someone older. This chapter will help you understand the difference between formal and informal Afrikaans, including how to choose the right tone, the right words, and how to be polite in different situations.

## What Is Formal and Informal Language?

Formal language is used in more serious or respectful situations. It shows politeness and respect, and you would use it when talking to someone older, someone in a position of authority, or in a professional setting. For example, you would speak formally to a teacher, a boss, or a stranger.

Informal language is used in casual conversations with friends, family, or people you know well. It's more relaxed, and you don't need to worry as much about using polite phrases or specific grammar rules. You might speak informally with your classmates, siblings, or close friends.

## Formal Pronouns: "U" vs. Informal Pronouns: "Jy"

One of the biggest differences between formal and informal Afrikaans is the pronouns you use for "you." In Afrikaans, the formal way to say "you" is **u** (pronounced: oo), while the informal way is **jy** (pronounced: yay).

- **U** – This is the formal pronoun, used when talking to someone older, like a teacher, or in formal settings.

- **Jy** – This is the informal pronoun, used when talking to someone your own age, like a friend or classmate.

For example:

- **Hoe gaan dit met u?** (pronounced: hoo khahn dit met oo) – This means "How are you?" in a formal way.
- **Hoe gaan dit met jou?** (pronounced: hoo khahn dit met yow) – This means "How are you?" in an informal way.

Knowing when to use **u** or **jy** helps you show respect and adjust your tone for different situations.

## Politeness in Formal Language

Being polite is a big part of formal language. In formal situations, you need to use certain words and phrases to show respect. One important word is **asseblief** (pronounced: ah-suh-bleef), which means "please."

- **Mag ek asseblief met u praat?** (pronounced: mahkh ek ah-suh-bleef met oo praht) – This means "May I please speak with you?" It's a polite way to ask for permission in formal situations.

Other polite phrases you might use in formal situations include:

- **Dankie** (pronounced: dun-kee) – This means "thank you."
- **Verskoon my** (pronounced: fer-skohn may) – This means "excuse me" or "pardon me."

For example:

- **Dankie vir u hulp** (pronounced: dun-kee fer oo hulp) – This means "Thank you for your help" and is used in formal situations.

## Informal Language: Relaxed and Friendly

When talking with friends or family, you can use informal language, which is much more relaxed. You don't need to use **u** or polite phrases like **asseblief** as often, and you can speak in a more direct way.

- **Hoe gaan dit met jou?** – This is an informal way to ask, "How are you?" when talking to a friend.

Here are some informal words and phrases you can use in casual conversations:

- **Hallo** (pronounced: hah-loh) – This means "hello" and is used in both formal and informal settings, but more often in informal conversations.

- **Hey** – This is an even more informal way to say "hi" to a friend.

- **Dis cool** (pronounced: dis kool) – This means "That's cool" and is used in casual conversations with friends.

In informal conversations, you can be more casual and friendly. You don't need to worry as much about being polite or formal.

## Choosing the Right Tone

The tone of your voice and the words you use are important in both formal and informal settings. Choosing the right tone helps you communicate effectively and respectfully in different situations. Here are some tips for choosing the right tone:

- **Use a polite and respectful tone when speaking to teachers, adults, or people you don't know well.** Even if you're using simple words, your tone should show respect.

- **Use a friendly and relaxed tone when speaking with friends and family.** You can be more casual, and it's okay to laugh or use slang.

For example, when speaking to a teacher, you might say:

- **Kan ek asseblief u vra?** (pronounced: kahn ek ah-suh-bleef oo frah) – This means "Can I please ask you?" in a formal tone.

But when talking to a friend, you might say:

- **Kan ek jou vra?** (pronounced: kahn ek yow frah) – This means "Can I ask you?" in a casual tone.

## Titles in Formal Language

In formal Afrikaans, it's important to use titles when addressing adults or people in authority. Here are some common titles:

- **Meneer** (pronounced: muh-neer) – This means "Mr." and is used to address a man formally.

- **Mevrou** (pronounced: meh-frow) – This means "Mrs." and is used to address a married woman.

- **Juffrou** (pronounced: yuh-frow) – This means "Miss" or "Teacher" and is often used to address female teachers.

Here's an example of how you would use these titles in a sentence:

- **Goeie môre, Meneer** (pronounced: ghoy-uh mor-ruh muh-neer) – This means "Good morning, Sir." It's a polite way to greet a man formally.

## Using "Please" and "Thank You"

Whether you're speaking formally or informally, it's always important to use polite phrases like "please" and "thank you." However, in formal conversations, you need to use these phrases more often to show respect.

- **Asseblief** – Use this word whenever you're asking for something in a formal setting.

- **Dankie** – Say "thank you" to show gratitude, especially in formal situations.

In informal conversations, you can still use these phrases, but you don't need to be as formal. For example, you might say:

- **Kan ek die boek hê?** (pronounced: kahn ek dee book heh) – This means "Can I have the book?" It's polite but informal because you're not using **asseblief**.

## Formal and Informal Writing

Just like speaking, writing in Afrikaans can be formal or informal. When writing a letter or email to a teacher or someone in authority, you should use formal language. Here's an example of a formal way to start a letter:

- **Geagte Meneer** (pronounced: ghuh-ahkh-tuh muh-neer) – This means "Dear Sir" and is used in formal writing.

In informal writing, like sending a message to a friend, you can be more relaxed. For example:

- **Hallo, hoe gaan dit?** – This means "Hello, how are you?" and is a casual way to start a conversation with a friend.

## Key Points to Remember

- **Formal pronouns**: Use **u** when speaking to someone older or in authority, and **jy** for friends and peers.

- **Politeness**: In formal conversations, use words like **asseblief** and **dankie** to show respect.

- **Titles**: Address people formally using **Meneer** (Mr.), **Mevrou** (Mrs.), or **Juffrou** (Miss/Teacher).

- **Informal language**: In casual conversations, you can use shorter phrases, slang, and a more relaxed tone.

- **Choosing tone**: Use a formal tone in professional settings, and a friendly tone when talking to friends or family.

# Chapter 44

# Advanced Conversation: Debates and Discussions

As you become more comfortable with Afrikaans, you'll start having more advanced conversations. This includes talking about different opinions, debating, and discussing ideas. In this chapter, we'll learn how to have a conversation in Afrikaans that involves expressing your opinion, agreeing or disagreeing, and asking questions to learn more. Being able to debate and discuss is important because it helps you communicate better with others and share your thoughts confidently.

## Expressing Your Opinion

One of the first steps in a discussion is learning how to express your opinion. In Afrikaans, there are a few different ways to say what you think. Here are some common phrases to use when you want to give your opinion:

- **Ek dink...** (pronounced: ek dink) – This means "I think..." and is a simple way to start sharing your opinion.

- **Na my mening...** (pronounced: nah may mee-ning) – This means "In my opinion..." and is a more formal way of expressing your thoughts.

- **Ek glo...** (pronounced: ek gloh) – This means "I believe..." and is used when you want to express a strong opinion or belief.

Here are some examples of how you might use these phrases in a discussion:

- **Ek dink ons moet meer lees** (pronounced: ek dink ohns moot meer lees) – This means "I think we should read more."

- **Na my mening is dit belangrik om te oefen** (pronounced: nah may mee-ning is dit buh-lahng-rik om tuh oo-fen) – This means "In my opinion, it is important to exercise."

- **Ek glo dat almal moet respek hê vir ander** (pronounced: ek gloh daht ahl-mahl moot rehs-pek heh fer ahn-der) – This means "I believe that everyone should have respect for others."

When you're sharing your opinion, it's important to be clear and confident. Using these phrases can help you start a discussion and let others know what you think.

## Agreeing with Someone

In a debate or discussion, you may agree with what someone else says. In Afrikaans, there are different ways to show agreement. Here are some phrases to use when you agree with someone's opinion:

- **Ek stem saam** (pronounced: ek stem sahm) – This means "I agree." It's a simple and direct way to show agreement.

- **Ek dink jy is reg** (pronounced: ek dink yay is rekh) – This means "I think you are right." It's a polite way to agree and also compliment the other person's idea.

- **Ek stem heeltemal saam** (pronounced: ek stem heel-teh-mahl sahm) – This means "I completely agree." Use this when you strongly agree with someone.

For example:

- **Ek stem saam dat dit goed is om gesond te eet** (pronounced: ek stem sahm daht dit khoot is om ghuh-sont tuh eet) – This means "I agree that it is good to eat healthy."

When you agree with someone, it's important to let them know so that you can build on their idea and continue the discussion in a positive way.

## Disagreeing Politely

Sometimes, in a discussion, you might not agree with what someone else is saying. It's okay to disagree, but it's important to do so politely. Here are some ways to disagree with someone in Afrikaans without being rude:

- **Ek stem nie saam nie** (pronounced: ek stem nee sahm nee) – This means "I don't agree." It's a simple way to express disagreement without being disrespectful.

- **Ek sien dit anders** (pronounced: ek seen dit ahn-ders) – This means "I see it differently." This is a polite way to show that you have a different opinion.

- **Ek verstaan wat jy sê, maar...** (pronounced: ek fer-staan vaht yay say mahr) – This means "I understand what you're saying, but..." It's a way to acknowledge someone's opinion while offering a different perspective.

For example:

- **Ek stem nie saam nie, want ek dink dit is te moeilik** (pronounced: ek stem nee sahm nee vahnt ek dink dit is tuh moo-ee-lik) – This means "I don't agree, because I think it's too difficult."

When you disagree politely, it keeps the conversation respectful and allows everyone to share their ideas without feeling hurt or upset.

## Asking Questions in a Discussion

In any discussion, asking questions is a great way to learn more about someone else's opinion. It shows that you are interested in what they are saying and want to understand their point of view. Here are some helpful phrases for asking questions in Afrikaans:

- **Hoekom dink jy so?** (pronounced: hoo-kom dink yay soh) – This means "Why do you think so?" It's a good way to ask for more explanation.

- **Kan jy meer verduidelik?** (pronounced: kahn yay meer fer-dow-duh-lik) – This means "Can you explain more?" It's a polite way to ask for more information.

- **Hoe voel jy daaroor?** (pronounced: hoo feel yay dahr-oor) – This means "How do you feel about that?" It's a way to ask for someone's personal opinion or feelings.

For example:

- **Hoekom dink jy dat ons meer moet lees?** (pronounced: hoo-kom dink yay daht ohns meer moot lees) – This means "Why do you think we should read more?" It's a way to ask for more reasoning behind someone's opinion.

Asking questions helps keep the conversation going and allows you to understand others better.

## Giving Reasons for Your Opinion

In a discussion or debate, it's not enough to just say what you think. You also need to explain why you think that way. This is called giving reasons or supporting your opinion. In Afrikaans, you can use these phrases to explain your reasons:

- **Ek dink so omdat...** (pronounced: ek dink soh om-daht) – This means "I think so because..." It's a way to explain your reasoning.

- **Die rede hoekom ek so voel is...** (pronounced: dee reh-duh hoo-kom ek soh feel is) – This means "The reason why I feel this way is..." It's another way to give reasons for your opinion.

For example:

- **Ek dink ons moet meer oefen omdat dit goed is vir ons gesondheid** (pronounced: ek dink ohns moot meer oo-fen om-daht dit khoot is fer ohns ghuh-sond-heid) – This means "I think we should exercise more because it's good for our health."

Giving reasons for your opinion makes your argument stronger and helps others understand your point of view better.

## Ending a Discussion Respectfully

At the end of a discussion, it's important to finish the conversation politely, especially if people have different opinions. Here are some ways to end a discussion respectfully:

- **Ek waardeer jou opinie** (pronounced: ek vahr-deer yow oh-pee-nee) – This means "I appreciate your opinion." It's a polite way to show that you respect someone's thoughts, even if you don't agree.

- **Dis goed om verskillende menings te hê** (pronounced: dis khoot om fer-skil-len-deh mee-nings tuh heh) – This means "It's good to have different opinions." This phrase shows that you understand and accept that everyone can have their own view.

For example:

- **Ek waardeer jou opinie, maar ek dink anders** (pronounced: ek vahr-deer yow oh-pee-nee mahr ek dink ahn-ders) – This means "I appreciate your opinion, but I think differently."

Ending a discussion in a respectful way helps everyone feel valued, even if they have different viewpoints.

## Key Points to Remember

- **Expressing opinions**: Use phrases like **Ek dink...** or **Na my mening...** to share your opinion clearly.

- **Agreeing politely**: You can say **Ek stem saam** to show that you agree with someone's opinion.

- **Disagreeing politely**: Use **Ek stem nie saam nie** or **Ek sien dit anders** to disagree respectfully.

- **Asking questions**: Use **Hoekom dink jy so?** to ask why someone thinks a certain way and encourage more discussion.

- **Giving reasons**: Use **Ek dink so omdat...** to give reasons for your opinion and explain your thinking.

# Chapter 45

# Conclusion and Further Learning

Congratulations on completing this book! You have learned a lot about Afrikaans, from the basic alphabet and sounds to more complex grammar, conversation skills, and cultural traditions. Learning a new language is a great way to understand another culture and communicate with people from different backgrounds. Although this book has introduced you to the essentials of Afrikaans, there is always more to learn. In this chapter, we'll discuss what you've accomplished so far and offer suggestions for resources and tips to help you continue your learning journey.

## What You've Learned

By working through this book, you now have a solid foundation in Afrikaans. Here's a quick recap of what you've covered:

- **The Afrikaans Alphabet and Pronunciation:** You learned how to read and pronounce Afrikaans letters and sounds, including vowels and consonants.

- **Basic Greetings and Introductions:** You practiced saying hello, introducing yourself, and making simple conversations.

- **Numbers, Days, and Telling Time:** You mastered counting, telling time, and talking about days of the week and months of the year.

- **Sentence Structure:** You learned how to form sentences using the Subject-Verb-Object (SVO) structure in Afrikaans.

- **Grammar:** You explored important grammar rules like using verbs, nouns, pronouns, and adjectives in your sentences.

- **Cultural Traditions and Expressions:** You discovered some key aspects of Afrikaans culture and learned common idioms and sayings.

Now that you have this strong base, it's time to think about how to keep improving your Afrikaans skills. In the next sections, we'll explore different ways to continue learning.

## Practicing with Native Speakers

One of the best ways to improve your language skills is by practicing with native Afrikaans speakers. Talking with someone who speaks the language fluently helps you get used to hearing and understanding Afrikaans in real-life situations. You can also learn the natural flow of conversation and pick up on cultural nuances that aren't always covered in books.

Here are a few ways to practice with native speakers:

- **Online language exchange platforms:** There are many websites and apps where you can find people from around the world who want to practice languages. You can practice Afrikaans with native speakers while helping them practice English!

- **Join local language groups:** Some cities and towns have language clubs or meetups where people gather to practice different languages. Check to see if there's an Afrikaans-speaking group near you.

- **Find a pen pal:** Writing letters or emails to a pen pal who speaks Afrikaans is a fun way to practice your reading and writing skills while also making a new friend.

The more you practice, the more confident you'll become in your ability to communicate in Afrikaans.

## Watching Afrikaans Movies and TV Shows

Watching movies and TV shows in Afrikaans is a great way to improve your listening skills and become more familiar with how the language is spoken in everyday life. You'll get to hear how people use the language in different contexts, from casual conversations to more formal situations.

Here are some tips for getting the most out of watching Afrikaans content:

- **Start with subtitles:** When you're just starting out, it's okay to watch with English subtitles. Over time, as you become more comfortable, try watching with Afrikaans subtitles or no subtitles at all.

- **Pause and repeat:** If you don't understand a word or phrase, pause the video and try to figure it out. You can even rewind and listen again to practice hearing the sounds and pronunciation.

- **Choose different genres:** Watching a variety of genres, like dramas, comedies, or documentaries, will expose you to different types of conversations and vocabulary.

Some popular Afrikaans TV shows and movies include:

- **7de Laan** – A popular Afrikaans soap opera that's great for picking up everyday vocabulary and casual conversation styles.
- **Die Pro** – A coming-of-age movie set in South Africa that features Afrikaans dialogue and cultural themes.

## Listening to Afrikaans Music and Podcasts

Music is another fun way to immerse yourself in the Afrikaans language. Listening to Afrikaans songs can help you improve your pronunciation and learn new vocabulary. Many Afrikaans songs also reflect cultural stories and values, so you'll learn more about the culture as well.

Here are some ways to use music and podcasts to improve your Afrikaans:

- **Find Afrikaans music artists:** Look up popular Afrikaans music artists like **Die Heuwels Fantasties** or **Jack Parow**. Listen to their songs and try to follow along with the lyrics.
- **Use music apps:** Many apps like Spotify or YouTube allow you to create playlists of Afrikaans songs so you can listen and practice while doing other things.
- **Listen to Afrikaans podcasts:** There are many podcasts available where native Afrikaans speakers discuss various topics. Find one that interests you and listen regularly to improve your understanding of spoken Afrikaans.

## Reading Afrikaans Books and Articles

Reading in Afrikaans is a fantastic way to build your vocabulary and improve your grammar. When you read books or articles in Afrikaans, you can see how sentences are structured and learn new words in context.

Here are some tips for reading in Afrikaans:

- **Start with children's books:** Even though you're older, children's books are a great way to ease into reading Afrikaans. The language is simpler, and the stories are engaging.
- **Read short stories and articles:** Once you feel more comfortable, you can move on to

short stories or online articles. Many websites offer news and entertainment content in Afrikaans, which can help you practice reading different types of writing.

- **Use a dictionary:** Keep an Afrikaans-English dictionary handy so you can look up any words you don't understand. Over time, you'll rely on the dictionary less as you expand your vocabulary.

## Taking Afrikaans Classes

If you want to continue learning Afrikaans in a more structured way, you might consider taking formal classes. Many schools, community centers, and online platforms offer language courses that can help you improve your skills.

- **Enroll in an online course:** Websites like Udemy, Duolingo, or Coursera offer Afrikaans language courses that you can take at your own pace.

- **Join a local class:** Check if your local community college or language school offers Afrikaans classes. Learning in a classroom setting with a teacher can be very helpful for practicing speaking and getting feedback on your progress.

Taking classes allows you to have a teacher guide you through the learning process and answer any questions you have along the way.

## Set Language Learning Goals

One of the best ways to stay motivated as you continue learning Afrikaans is to set clear goals. Whether you want to learn a certain number of new words each week, have a conversation with a native speaker, or read a full book in Afrikaans, having goals will help you stay focused.

Here are some examples of language learning goals:

- **Learn 5 new Afrikaans words every day.**

- **Have a conversation in Afrikaans for at least 5 minutes.**

- **Watch a full episode of a TV show in Afrikaans without subtitles.**

As you meet your goals, you'll feel more confident in your abilities and be motivated to keep learning!

Made in the USA
Monee, IL
08 July 2025